Strikes, Lockouts and Super Bowl

Strikes, Lockouts and Super Bowl

INSIDE AMERICAN FOOTBALL

RHONDA SMITH

HEINEMANN KINGSWOOD

Heinemann Kingswood
Michelin House, 81 Fulham Road, London SW3 6RB

LONDON   MELBOURNE   AUCKLAND

Copyright © 1988 Rhonda V. Smith
First published 1988

ISBN 0 434 98168 0

Printed and bound in Great Britain by
Richard Clay Ltd, Bungay, Suffolk

For Moma and Chelsea

Acknowledgements

Special thanks to Daddy, Glenn, Rod and Regina, Mike Davis, Dick Bass, Derek Wyatt, Aunt T, Rondal, DeJuana, Tommy and Jamaal – it's time.

'I wondered as I sat there, if the millions who see football every year have any idea of the drama connected with it.'

— Corinne Griffith

Chapter One

On the evening that the National Football League players ended their 24-day strike against the NFL owners and management, ABC News reporter Ted Koppel interviewed Gene Upshaw, executive director of the players' union, on 'Nightline', a nationally televised news programme that focuses on the leading story or stories of the day. It had a rather ironic twist to it, in that the second story on the show was about a little girl in Midland, Texas, named Jessica McClure.

Eighteen-month-old Jessica had somehow fallen 22 feet below the ground down an abandoned well. The well's opening was only eight inches in diameter, and the entire country held its collective breath as hundreds of volunteers attempted to rescue her. Jessica was trapped in that well for two and a half days, without food or water; the sounds of drilling equipment, picks and shovels all around her. It was a test of endurance for her parents, for her rescuers, and most of all, for her. Everyone came through the experience with flying colours. Jessica is safe, and improving daily.

Her plight put the struggle between the players and the owners of the National Football League into a different perspective for me. While the issues were valid ones: money, job security, money, retirement benefits, money – their importance paled in comparison to Jessica's struggle to survive.

Still, the NFL strike was the headline story. Peoples' lives revolve around it. A portion of the population was so engrossed in its goings on that they didn't even know about Jessica. Football is an American obsession.

It's been that way for a very long time. Football has enjoyed a long, glorious history of over 100 years, complete with heroes and superstars, success and popularity, dissension and litigation, violence and gradual decline. Yet, the relationship between the National Football League and the American public is like a rock-solid marriage. Through thick and thin, as long as professional games are played, fan support – and dollars – will be right there.

The actual *game* of football is one of the more exciting, passionate spectator sports around. The level of physical competition, and the combined talents of the individual athletes, arouse the deepest aggression in football fans and followers. As your basic, maniacal 'football fanatic', I personally consider the game a great way to release pent-up aggression – second only to a five-mile run, sex, or kicking the dog.

It all started in 19th-century England. There, William Webb Ellis, a student at Rugby School, picked up the ball during a soccer game and ran with it. The rules of the game forbade advancing the ball in any way except kicking it, and this infraction outraged many of the soccer purists. It became, however, the basis of a new game that would be called rugby, and would be a forerunner of modern American football.

In the American colonies, Boston high schools played soccer football games against each other in 1860. And, on 6 November 1862, Rutgers and Princeton played each other in a game that vaguely resembled football as we know it today, marking the beginning of organised college football. Yale, Columbia and Harvard all had soccer football teams. Harvard's game, however, was called the 'Boston Game' and was more closely akin to rugby. McGill University of Montreal, Canada, played rugby, and in 1874 played three games against Harvard. As a result, Harvard changed its game completely to rugby rather than soccer, instituting the principles of running with the ball and tackling.

It seemed for a while that each school had a different set of rules. The sport was in a state of total confusion. Then, following the lead of the London Football Association (which, organised in 1862, marked the beginning of rules conventions – a sports tradition), the first rules for American football (rugby football) were written at the Massasoit convention of 1876, held in Springfield, Massachusetts.

In that same year, Walter Camp, who would become known as the 'father of modern football', entered Yale University. He played halfback in rugby football, and among other achievements, represented his university at the annual rules convention in 1877, as a sophomore. Camp remained a force in the refinement of the game for many years to come. Some of his contributions include: the creation of the positions of 'quarterback' and 'snapback' (centre); a rule requiring a team to advance the ball five yards in three downs (later increased to ten yards in four downs); and in 1888, a rule permitting tackling as low as the knees.

College football was exceedingly popular. But, in the years that followed, it became a dangerous, brutal sport. Fighting increased, and there were deaths on the field. A public outcry led President Theodore Roosevelt to call a White House conference in 1905, and tell the school representatives to clean up football. This in turn led to the formation of the Intercollegiate Athletic Association, later known as the National Collegiate Athletic Association (NCAA). Walter Camp and his associates in the NCAA defined the game that the National Football League would adapt in 1920, and not change for more than ten years.

In 1868, the New York Athletic Club was formed, the first of its kind. After that, athletic clubs sprang up in virtually every eastern American city. Though all were presumed to be amateurs, some clubs were known to bend the rules. William (Pudge) Heffelfinger, of the Allegheny Athletic Association of Pittsburgh (Pennsylvania), received payment to play football in 1892, and is deemed the first professional player. His payment, despite being 'under the table', began the recorded history of professional football. Once athletic clubs dropped the pretence of being amateurs, professional clubs rose and fell all over the northeast. In 1899, the Duquesne Country and Athletic Club found itself stretched to its financial limit by a huge payroll. So it turned to William Chase Temple, a wealthy industrialist, for help. He bought the team from the athletic club and became professional football's first individual owner.

Hundreds of exceptionally talented athletes have played the game of football over the years. In its early days, the Saturday afternoon heroes came from the college ranks. One of the first of such stars, and without question the greatest of his time, was Jim Thorpe, a native American. During the beginning of the 20th century, Thorpe played halfback at the Carlisle Indian Industrial School in Carlisle, Pennsylvania. In 1912, he represented the United States in the fifth Olympiad, where he won the decathlon and the pentathlon, prompting King Gustav V to say to him, 'Sir, you are the greatest athlete in the world.' His professional career began in 1915, when he signed with the Canton (Ohio) Bulldogs. And, in 1920, Jim

3

Thorpe represented the Bulldogs at the organisational meeting of a new league, and was named its charter president.

Ah, for the good ole days! Things were so simple then. On 17 September 1920 ten men gathered in the garage of the Hay Motor Company in Canton, Ohio, and formed the American Professional Football Association.

They represented teams from Ohio, Pennsylvania, New York and Indiana. The franchise fee was $100 but, since no treasury records were kept, it is not known if all of the owners paid up.

The league was reorganised in 1921, and Joe Carr, general manager of the Columbus Panhandlers, was elected president, replacing Jim Thorpe. Later in the year, a franchise was granted to Green Bay, Wisconsin. The 1921 season is the first listed as having produced standings (results tables) and a recognised champion. The Decatur Staleys, owned by George Halas, won the championship. Then, early in 1922, the Staleys moved to Chicago, and the team was renamed the Chicago Bears. That same year, the American Professional Football Association was renamed the National Football League.

Another superstar of those early years was Red Grange. Known as the 'Galloping Ghost', Grange had earned a reputation at the Univerisity of Illinois as a great runner. George Halas, astute businessman that he was, recognised a goldmine when he saw one, and, in September 1925, quickly signed Grange to play for the Chicago Bears. Thus began the American love affair with professional football. Red Grange was one of the game's biggest box-office attractions. At one game in New York, 20,000 fans were turned away because the stadium was already overflowing with 70,000 people. He was paid $30,000 for that one game (his contract included a large share of the gate). In time, Grange and his agent, Charles C. (Cash and Carry) Pyle, came to realise the tremendous impact the 'Galloping Ghost', was having on the game. So, Pyle went to George Halas and demanded that Grange be given part ownership in the Bears. When Halas refused, Grange and Pyle formed their own league. The American Football League, the first of six rival leagues to challenge the NFL (four of which were called the American Football League), was built around Grange. Some of the top professional players of the decade were lured over, but the overall picture was a financial disaster, and both Grange and Pyle lost heavily.

The NFL grew and prospered over the next three decades. As rival leagues came and went, the game was continually polished and refined. By 1940, the cost of a franchise was $50,000, and the only small town remaining in the league was Green Bay. By the 1950s, the league was setting new attendance records, several television stations were broadcasting games, and gross receipts from radio were higher than ever. The NFL was rapidly becoming a very exclusive fraternity. So exclusive, in fact, that two wealthy Texans (sons of wealthy Texas oilmen), frustrated at their inability to obtain NFL franchises, met with six other equally frustrated, wealthy men in August 1959, and formed the American Football League (No. 4). The franchise fee was $100,000 (everyone paid). With very deep pockets, and the willingness and ability to persevere, the AFL then waged pro football's longest war, and became the NFL's most formidable foe.

In 1960, Pete Rozelle, a 'public relations wizard', was named commissioner of the NFL. Two years later, he negotiated a single season television contract with the Columbia Broadcasting System (CBS) for $4.6 million.

Joe Foss, once governor of South Dakota, and a Congressional Medal of Honour winner, was named the AFL's first commissioner. In 1964, he negotiated a lucrative five-year television contract with the National Broadcasting Company (NBC) worth $36 million. It was the turning point for his young league.

But it was Pete Rozelle, more than anyone else in the business, who was the acknowledged architect of this nation's obsession with watching professional football. When he took office, the NFL had 12 teams. He fought a noble battle with the AFL, then successfully merged the two leagues. Today, the NFL has 28 teams (with plans to expand in the very near future) and sells many millions more tickets than it did in 1960. Back then, an average franchise was worth $2 million. Today, an average franchise is worth over $50 million.

Pete Rozelle sensed Americans' need 'to identify with ritualised physical confrontation', and he understood exactly how to capitalise on that need. In 1982, he negotiated a five-year contract with the three major networks – NBC, CBS and ABC (American Broadcasting Company) – totalling over $2 *billion*. 'I think it's the action,' he says. 'Americans love action, and football is well suited to television.' Of American television's ten most watched sports events of all time, all ten are NFL games. Rozelle took what journalist David Harris called 'a muddy, mildly popular game played mostly in ancient stadiums and televised sporadically in black and white, and shaped it into a national addiction fought in sleek new football palaces, on a surface like a billiard table and televised everywhere . . . He made it easy and exciting for everyone to become a fan.'

In 1984, Pete said: 'It is very important that we keep the public emotionally involved and caring enough to watch on television and to buy tickets to the stadium . . . But to a great extent, the product carries itself. We have a hold on the public that I don't envisage going significantly downhill.' Ironically, those words came at a time when the 'hold' was more precarious than ever before. It had begun to slip – ever so slightly – in 1970; then a bit more in 1974. By 1980, Pete appeared to be coming apart at the seams; and by 1982 some felt he had already lost it.

1970 was the first year that the NFL and AFL operated as a single entity, and the last year that Pete Rozelle played a significant role in contract negotiations between the players' union and the owners. (The union was formed in 1956, and its history is described in Chapter 3.) When stalled talks led to a players' boycott of preseason training camps, Pete fancied himself the ideal arbitrator, because he was 'an impartial representative of the entire game'. But the players wanted nothing to do with his mediation. During the final negotiating session, whenever the two sides took a break, Pete would leave with the owners. 'If you're so goddamn neutral,' union president John Mackey complained, 'why do you always leave with them?' The last meeting went on for 22 straight hours before an agreement was finally reached. The union felt there was no winner. The owners, they said, 'gave us nothing'. The commissioner, however, was credited by the press with having 'locked the two sides in a room together and forced them to find an agreement'. Union executive director Ed Garvey called that account 'bullshit'.

In 1974, the union still carried the grudge of the 'failed' negotiations of 1970. They vowed solidarity for the '74 talks, and set their sights on 'freedom issues', including elimination

6

of the commissioner's authority to discipline players, the banning of all psychological and personality testing, creation of total free agency for players, and elimination of the Rozelle Rule affecting players' transfer to other teams (see p. 12). As in 1970, talks stalled and picket lines appeared at training camps around the League. But the players' 'unity' disappeared, and their strike collapsed. They returned to work without an agreement, then rebounded by pursuing a lawsuit that would keep the League in court for over three years. The decision in that case (Mackey vs. NFL) was called a 'catastrophe on the League's labour front' by one owner. Ruling in favour of the union, the court struck down the Rozelle Rule as 'unreasonable' and 'clearly contrary to public policy'.

But wait! It gets worse!

When the Los Angeles Rams left the L.A. Coliseum and moved to Anaheim in 1980, Al Davis, managing general partner of the Oakland Raiders (and Pete Rozelle's only known *genuine* enemy amongst the team owners), announced that he would be moving his team south into the vacated Los Angeles Memorial Coliseum. Hold on, Pete said. You can't do that without approval from the League members. Up yours, said Al, who had forseen that his bid for independence would rile Pete, I don't need, and am not going to ask for permission to move my team. If you don't like it, you can try and stop me! Thus began what was called 'the most decisive battle in National Football League history'.

The League attempted to block the Raiders' move through lawsuits and restraining orders. But Al not only proceeded with his team's move, he filed suit against the League (and Pete Rozelle specifically) citing violations of the antitrust laws, and asking for $160 million in damages. (Antitrust (monopolies) laws have been the bugbear of American football for 20 years and how they affect it is explained in Chapter 2.) The trial was long, costly, very ugly and extremely damaging to the image and credibility of the National Football League. 'League Think', Pete Rozelle's philosophy of unfettered unity, was publicly shot to hell. The courts ruled in favour of Al Davis, and ordered the League to pay him $11.5 million, which was tripled under antitrust laws; plus $10 million in legal fees – nearly $50 million. It was a severe blow to the NFL; the first time in almost 25 years that Commissioner Rozelle had ever cost it money.

1982 was the worst year to date for American professional football. Still reeling from nearly ten years of litigation, the NFL was now facing a workers/management battle that would spawn a 57-day work stoppage by the players, and later be described as 'a landmark of financial devastation'. Everyone lost – players, owners, stadiums, cities. Bad industrial relations was a fact. And the public's distaste for the whole situation was evidenced by reduced attendance for the second half of the season, as well as reduced televison ratings. After half a decade of lawsuits and the worst industrial war in its history, there was now little doubt that the National Football League was first and foremost a business. With that conclusion, much of the mystique PR expert Pete Rozelle had spent two decades building crumbled in a heap at his feet.

It took the American public quite a while to come back round after the 1982 strike. The smaller crowds and lower ratings continued into 1983, '84 and '85. The television bonanza, which had fuelled football's dramatic rise in popularity, began to disappear. 'What had once seemed an insatiable demand for whatever the league broadcast, was suddenly proving significantly less marketable,' as David Harris noted. Advertisers, who had been paying over $200,000 per minute for NFL broadcast time, were understandably upset.

With the 1983 arrival of the United States Football League, an experiment in spring football, support for the professional game in America appeared to have reached the saturation point. By the beginning of 1986, NFL football was a 'network money-loser'. In an attempt to turn this deterioration around, and put 'League Think' back together, Commissioner Rozelle went to Washington DC, as he had many times before during the past 20 years, to lobby the US Congress for an exemption from antitrust laws. But he found that his 'once magical Congressional touch' had disappeared, and that in order to secure any possibility of results, the NFL had to be prepared to consider expanding into cities hungry for professional football, especially those represented by powerful members of Congress. Pete, however, was unable to commit to expansion without the owners' approval, and the owners were not inclined to approve a move which would mean dividing television revenue more ways. So Pete was faced with another stalemate.

8

As he doggedly attempts to return the game to its glory days, to its 1981 zenith of popularity, Commissioner Alvin 'Pete' Rozelle laments, 'This job is not as much fun as it once was.'

Chapter Two

If you are going to understand the National Football League Players' Association's 1987 work stoppage against the League's owners, or the strike of 1982, or the precedent-setting lawsuit of <u>Mackey vs. National Football League</u>, you must first understand American antitrust law, known as the Sherman Act. It seems that the bottom line of every argument I've ever heard in the business of professional football is some violation of the Sherman Act. Its application to professional sports, however, appears to be filled with loopholes, and is constantly challenged. Baseball, for instance, is exempt from antitrust laws. Football has spent hundreds of thousands of dollars seeking a similar status. The NFL, represented by Rozelle, has lobbied Congress not only for an exemption, but for a *retroactive* exemption, so that the ruling in every case lost so far would be reversed!

Defined simply as a statute 'to protect trade and commerce against unlawful restraints and monopolies', the Sherman Act was based on the Common Law, which the United States inherited from England. It is widely believed that this body of judicial decisions always favoured freedom of trade. At the end of the 19th century, many United States senators, aware that discoveries and inventions had caused dramatic increases in trade, contracts, and corporations, could foresee that, unchecked, these increases might ultimately put most of the property evolved by the workforce into the hands of a small minority of men. They felt that the best way to prevent 'the crafty and strong minority from combining to extort high prices for commodities from the weaker and uncombined majority of people', was by law. So, at the end of 1889, Senator John Sherman proposed such a law, and pushed it with such vigour that it was enacted by Congress with only one opposing vote, and approved by President Harrison on 2 July 1890.

As written in the law books, the principle provisions of the Sherman Act are: 'Sec. 1) Every contract, combination in the form of trust or otherwise, or conspiracy, in restraint of trade or commerce among the several States, or with foreign nations, is declared to be illegal. . . . Every person who shall make any contract or engage in any combination or conspiracy declared . . . to be illegal shall be deemed guilty of a misdemeanour. . . . Sec. 2) Every person who shall monopolise, or combine or conspire with any other person or persons, to monopolise any part of trade or commerce among the several States, or with foreign nations, shall be deemed guilty of a mis-demeanour. . . .' The law further provides that plaintiffs who have established a substantive antitrust violation ('any person . . . injured in his business or property, by reason of anything forbidden in the antitrust laws . . .') may recover treble damages.

The broad scope of the law was summed up years later in the decision of the 1958 case of Northern Pacific Railway Co. vs. United States: 'The Sherman Act was designed to be a comprehensive charter of economic liberty aimed at preserving free and unfettered competition as the rule of trade. It rests on the premise that the unrestrained interaction of competitive forces will yield the best allocation of our economic resources, the lowest prices, the highest quality and the greatest material progress, while at the same time producing an environment conducive to the preservation of our democratic, political and social institutions. But even were that premise open to question, the policy unequivocally laid down by the Act is competition.'

Baseball, America's 'national pastime', was the first professional sport in which an effort was made to apply federal anti-trust laws. In the 1922 case of Federal Baseball Club of Baltimore vs. National League of Professional Baseball Clubs, the Supreme Court ruled that baseball was not interstate commerce, and granted it total exemption from the Sherman Act, a privilege it has now enjoyed through most of its history. When the decision was challenged in the 1953 case of Toolson vs. New York Yankees, the court upheld it, arguing that, 'since Congress had done nothing to change the situation since 1922, it had intended baseball to have an exemption.' Theoretically protected from the threat of competition for players both from without (rival leagues) and from within (each other), baseball is still faced with the internal issues of franchise movement, rules changes and broadcasting policy, all of which require

11

majority votes from member clubs. Disagreement within a cartel (an organisation in an industry, such as an organisation of sports teams, which limits competition and divides markets, and has no moral or legal connotations) often tends to produce instability.

Which brings us to the National Football League. Lacking the total antitrust exemption granted to baseball, professional football operates, nonetheless, in a monopolistic, anti-competitive business manner; such is the nature of the sports league. As a result, a great deal of its recent history has been written in the courts, and a great deal of its time and energy have been spent lobbying Congress.

In 1946, William Radovich, a guard with the Detroit Lions, asked to be traded to Los Angeles to be near his terminally ill father. He was refused, so he jumped to the rival All-America Football Conference. When the AAFC subsequently folded, Radovich was offered a coaching job in the NFL. But the League blocked the deal, and in 1957 found itself in court. In the case of William Radovich vs. National Football League, the plaintiff charged that, 'This blacklisting effectively prevented his employment in organised football and was the result of a conspiracy . . . to monopolise interstate commerce in professional football.' When the NFL argued that the same exemption granted baseball should likewise cover football, the Supreme Court disagreed, ruling that Congress, not the Court, had to make that decision.

Thus began the quest for a total exemption from the antitrust law. Commissioner Bert Bell (Pete Rozelle's predecessor) came close in 1959. After Bell's death, Rozelle took up the cause, but succeeded only in securing limited exemptions – in 1961, allowing the league to sell its broadcasting rights as a single entity and then divide the revenue equally; and in 1966, allowing the merger of the NFL and the AFL.

The League's next significant encounter with the law it was trying so desperately to escape came in 1972, with the filing of John Mackey et al vs. National Football League. Mackey, a tight end with the Baltimore Colts, and a former president of the players' union, challenged the Rozelle Rule, which provided that any team signing a player whose contract has expired with another team, must compensate the player's former team. The required compensation was 'a player of equal calibre, selected by the commissioner'. To justify the rule, the league cited maintenance of competitive balance, protection of scouting and development investments, and promotion of player continuity. Mackey charged, however, that the rule made competition between clubs for veteran (experienced) players virtually nonexistent, which in turn suppressed players' salaries. He asked that players be granted free agency, which would allow them to sell their services without the penalty of compensation.

The district court struck down the Rozelle Rule on 29 December, 1975, on the grounds that it deterred players from becoming free agents, deterred clubs from negotiating with and signing free agents, decreased players' bargaining position in contract negotiations, and denied players the right to sell their services on a free market, thereby decreasing salaries and interclub movement of players. The court's decision stated: 'The Rozelle Rule constitutes a *per se* violation of the antitrust laws . . . so clearly . . . it is illegal under the Sherman Act. It is also an unreasonable restraint of trade at common law. The Rozelle Rule is unreasonably broad in its application . . . [and] is further unreasonable in that there are no procedural safeguards with respect to its employment. There is no hearing or opportunity to be heard. . . . The Rozelle Rule is unreasonable in that it is unlimited in duration. It is a perpetual restriction on a player. . . . He is at no time truly free to negotiate for his services with any club. . . . The Court finds that the existence of the Rozelle Rule and the other restrictive devices on players have not had any material effect on competitive balance in the National Football League. . . . Elimination of the Rozelle Rule would have no significant immediate disruptive effect on professional football. . . . Elimination of the Rozelle Rule will not spell the end of the National Football League or even cause a decrease in the number of franchises in the National Football League.'

Naturally, the League appealed against the decision. And, on 18 October 1976, the appeals court upheld the ruling, affirming that the Rozelle Rule 'unreasonably restrains trade in violation of the Sherman Act'. The appeals court also ruled (remember this point – it comes up again) that if the Rozelle Rule were a condition specifically accepted in a collective bargaining agreement, 'such a labour contract would exempt the

13

arrangement from Sherman Act jurisdiction'. Wellington Mara, owner of the New York Giants, called the decision a 'catastrophe'. For Commissioner Rozelle, it was his most turbulent period to date. The Mackey case, he said, 'attacked the very structure of the game. It attacked the validity of the game'.

Well, if Pete thought that 1976 was 'the most turbulent period since [he became] commissioner and very likely in the history of the League . . .', it was only because he had not a clue of what was in store for him in the 1980s! The long-time simmering rivalry between Rozelle and Oakland Raiders general managing partner, Al 'I don't get in a fight I can't win' Davis came to an explosive climax with the 25 March 1980 filing of LAMCC and Oakland Raiders Ltd vs. National Football League, Alvin Pete Rozelle, Eugene V. Klein, and Georgia Rosenbloom (Frontiere).

Davis, the acknowledged 'rebel' of the NFL cartel, decided to move his football team from Oakland to Los Angeles. He also decided that the unanimous vote requirement for League approval of such a move constituted an illegal restraint of trade, violating antitrust laws, and was therefore irrelevant and unnecessary. He didn't ask for a vote. Further, he informed the League that he would not abide by the results of one. So, on 4 March 1980, Pete Rozelle and the other League members filed Philadelphia Eagles et al vs. Oakland Raiders Ltd, asking that Al Davis be restrained from relocating his franchise. Al responded on 25 March by joining the Los Angeles Memorial Coliseum Commission in its suit against the NFL, and naming specific individuals who he claimed 'conspired to violate his economic rights'. Then it became personal. Sportswriter David Harris states: 'By the beginning of 1981, LAMCC vs. NFL was as much blood feud as lawsuit. Each party saw it as an ultimate test of just what the League was, each claimed the other was bullying him, and both sides vowed to never allow themselves to be pushed around.' This battle was long, and bitter, and dirty. It shook the very foundation upon which the League was built, and left in its wake a legacy of near anarchy.

The fighting was nonstop, even before the first piece of testimony was given. The case was scheduled to be heard in Los Angeles, but the League sought a change of venue. Judge

14

Harry Pregerson denied the request, and jury selection began on 13 May. Testimony began the following week. The trial was expected to last four months, feature more than 100 witnesses, and cost at least $5 million in attorneys' fees before any possible appeals would be completed.

The parade of witnesses began with Pete Rozelle. Next was Eugene Klein (then owner of the San Diego Chargers), who suffered a massive heart attack immediately after testifying. (Klein later filed a 'malicious prosecution' lawsuit against Davis, claiming Davis's personal vendetta caused his heart attack. He asked for $3 million in actual damages and $30 million in punitive damages. Late in 1986, the Court found in favour of Klein. The damages award is still being appealed.) Georgia Frontiere followed Klein on the witness stand. During her testimony on 9 June, one of the jurors noticed that she was pausing and looking at her husband before answering questions. Dominic Frontiere, the juror observed, was moving his head, either up and down or sideways, and she was replying accordingly. After the juror informed the court clerk that the movements may have been signals, Judge Pregerson called Mr Frontiere to his chambers. After two hours of interviewing, however, the court concluded that nothing improper had taken place.

Al Davis took the witness stand after Georgia, and stayed there through 18 June. His performance was most impressive. Even the judge expressed (in private) that Davis was the best witness he had ever seen. As Al left the stand, Judge Pregerson said, 'I sort of hate to see you leave.' Al replied prophetically, 'I'll see you around.' During the next six weeks, the procession of NFL witnesses included Tex Schramm (Dallas Cowboys), Herman Sarkowsky (Seattle Seahawks), Chuck Sullivan (New England Patriots), and Art Modell (Cleveland Browns). Unfortunately for the League, there was a perception, according to the *Los Angeles Times*, that, 'The testimony of NFL witnesses has, at times, been more helpful to the other side than to their own.'

On 26 June the court dropped the charges against Pete Rozelle, Gene Klein and Georgia Frontiere for lack of evidence, but the trial continued. By 20 July, the *L.A. Times* reported, there was 'a growing impression among observers at the National Football League antitrust trial that the wind has shifted and that the NFL is now sailing more or less into the teeth of it.' The case was given to the jury to decide on 29 July. They deliberated for nearly two weeks. Then, on 11 August, the judge received damaging information about one of the jurors.

It seems that Thomas Gelker, a retired plastics manufacturer from Anaheim, had a cousin who had owned a team in the old World Football League. When they were informed of this, the attorneys for the plaintiffs, Joseph Alioto (former mayor of San Francisco) and Maxwell Belcher, argued that Gelker should be dismissed from the jury. The main criterion by which the jurors were selected was 'of having virtually no knowledge or interest in professional football and no relations or friends involved in the NFL'. Gelker himself, they argued, had concealed the information. Judge Pregerson then interviewed each juror individually. Gelker claimed he had not seen his cousin in ten years. Three other jurors said that Gelker had 'displayed extensive knowledge of football, though he had represented himself during jury selection as uninformed about the sport'. As he interviewed, the judge took a poll, and found the jury split, eight for the plaintiffs and two for the defence, one of which was Gelker. None of them believed a unanimous vote was possible. The jury was hung. On the evening of 13 August, Judge Pregerson declared a mistrial. David Harris wrote: 'The most decisive battle in the history of the NFL had ended in no decision and would have to be replayed.'

The next day, Al Davis charged that the NFL had 'planted' Gelker. 'I anticipated this type of thing; that the NFL would do anything it could to win. It's the law of the jungle. . . . I'm not trying to make anyone squirm – but if I did, I think it would be fun.'

Before the retrial began on 30 March 1982, Al Davis told *Sport* magazine that the fear of change was the basis of the League's arguments: 'It's ridiculous. It's the same lament we've heard from Rozelle and the other owners in the NFL for the last ten or 15 years. When Congress lifted the TV blackout (imposed at one time by the NFL to encourage fan attendance at matches), Rozelle told Congress it would destroy the home gate. On the contrary, it's grown. Every time one of our illegal rules is struck from our constitution, it's meant "doom" for the league. But in reality, it's always been a new

16

beginning and the NFL has become a better league. . . . It's
the old fear package, something that's typical of Rozelle.

'He had a nickname for a while, Sneaky Pete. He was called
that in the League and he knows that. And that's the way he
operates. . . . Rozelle is the most powerful man in professional
sports and he does not want to give up his power base. This
[trial] is a challenge to it. He tried to destroy my negotiations
in Oakland. He's sent me letters threatening disciplinary action
that would, in essence, take my team away from me. He's sent
letters to banks in Los Angeles, telling them not to loan me
any money. All of those things are personal, there's no question
about it. . . . The League has what we call its police force. It's
a thing that started out as a security force to protect the League
from gambling influences and things like that. Instead, it has
become a personal gestapo for the commissioner, which he
uses unfairly on owners and players. . . . He has used it to
threaten owners. And he has used it to look into people and
harass them. God, the investigations that we've gone through.
. . . My life has been gone over with a fine-toothed comb.

'He [Rozelle] said in court that he wanted it [Los Angeles]
for the owners, but a lot of them say that they never even
discussed it. They asked Tex Schramm on the stand. He never
heard of it. They asked Billy Sullivan and he never heard of it
either. I really don't think that I would have had any problems
if I wanted to move my team to Phoenix. I strongly believe
that he wanted the territory for himself. I have my perceptions
and I know Pete. Pete lived there, his family lived there. He
wants equity. He doesn't want to be an employee, to have his
salary docked. He's got older and he's reached a stage where
he wants to play tennis, be a big socialite.'

Davis believed that Rozelle's personal needs even affected
negotiations for the new television contract. 'It was my opinion
that we should have signed a shorter contract. But it was a
victory at the time and he watches his life very carefully on
victories. He wanted that $2 billion figure. It gives him a
power base with the networks that he wants very badly when
he has to influence Congress or the country on certain issues.
The League probably has the most massive media control of
any entity in America other than the President.'

For his part, Pete Rozelle continued to maintain his de-
corum and ignore Davis's sniping.

The second trial was considerably shorter than the first, and it was decisive. On 7 May the case was turned over to the jury for deliberation, which took only six hours. With the personal charges against Pete, Gene and Georgia dropped, they had only two counts to decide: (1) if the vote required for League approval of a franchise move was in violation of the Sherman Act, and (2) if the League had breached its contract of fair and good faith bargaining with Al. They decided in favour of Davis and the LAMCC on both counts. On 13 April they awarded Davis $11.5 million, and the LAMCC $4.9 million in damages. Trebled, the total bill was nearly $50 million. In addition, the League was ordered to pay the plaintiffs' $10 million in legal fees. The League appealed – and lost. LAMCC vs. NFL has definitely been the heaviest of the body blows the commissioner – and the NFL – have had to absorb.

Chapter Three

Over lunch one day, I asked Mike Davis, defensive back for the San Diego Chargers and a member of the NFLPA Executive Committee, how the union came to be. 'Economic theory had nothing to do with it,' he said. 'The players simply wanted clean uniforms.'

It started in Green Bay, Wisconsin, in 1956. The Packers were having two practice sessions a day (a morning workout, and one in the afternoon) in training camp. After the morning session, the players' uniforms were placed back in the lockers – dirt, sweat, and all – to be worn again in the afternoon. When their request to management for clean, dry uniforms was denied, 'the Packers called for leaguewide solidarity on clean laundry'. Later that year, ten players met in New York and formed the National Football League Players' Association.

Most owners were opposed to, and therefore would not recognise a player's union. But, in his attempts to secure an antitrust exemption, Commissioner Bert Bell found that the most common complaint from politicians was the League's status as a non-union employer. 'Bell promised to get the owners to change their stance and convened a meeting to raise the issue to his bosses. The response was less than overwhelming and most were content to let the meeting end without even bringing the union's status to a vote. With adjournment imminent, Art Rooney of the Pittsburgh Steelers took the floor and, according to his son, Dan, forced the issue to a vote. He was assisted by Carrol Rosenbloom. Pushed to the wall, the League voted ten to two in favour of recognition.'

Structurally, sports unions are unique among American unions. They set minimum salary levels and establish standard pay for exhibition games, but do not negotiate individual player contracts. Those are done on an 'independent contractor' basis between club, player, and player agent. The union's primary focus is on working conditions and retirement benefits.

In January 1970, the NFLPA 'revised' itself to represent members of both the AFL and the NFL in the newly merged League. Tight end John Mackey of the Baltimore Colts was elected president. In March, Mackey said he foresaw no problems in the upcoming negotiations. The players' concerns were increased benefits in the pension plan, working of the option clause in the standard player contract, a larger share of product licensing, training camp and preseason game pay, and severance pay. But problems did arise; talks stalled, and in early July the union ordered veterans not to report to training camp (scheduled to open on 14 July) until further notice.

Although no picket lines were formed, only 21 players reported to camp before the 3 August agreement was reached. In the final stages of negotiation, John Mackey brought in a Minneapolis law firm to help write the actual contract. Ed Garvey, a new employee with the firm, and recently graduated from the University of Wisconsin law school, was given the assignment. Mackey was so pleased with Garvey's work, that he hired him as the union's executive director. The executive committee confirmed his selection in May 1971. Kansas City Chiefs owner Lamar Hunt complained that things were never the same again: 'The whole philosophy changed with Garvey's arrival. Now anything management did had to be negative.'

Ed Garvey felt that he had inherited a weak union which was poorly matched against people who played for keeps. It is widely believed that he was the catalyst behind the filing of Mackey vs. NFL, and by 1974, most of the League's owners considered him anything from an obnoxious nuisance to a dire threat. 'Even when they could agree on little else,' wrote Harris, 'from the time Mackey vs. NFL was filed, the mention of Ed Garvey's name alone was enough to turn most NFL conversations unanimously ugly.' He had hounded the League's flanks, smudged its image, cost it money, and provided the owners with someone besides each other to hate.

When the contract on which Garvey had done his first work expired in 1974, elimination of the Rozelle Rule was the union's major demand. 'To Garvey it was a legacy of subjugation with which he intended to break once and for all.' Baltimore Colts linebacker Bill Curry, the new NFLPA president, opened the first negotiating session with 'encouraging' remarks. Then Garvey read the following statement: 'It has been

20

four years since we looked across the bargaining table at one another. We have not forgotten the way you conducted yourself during the 1970 negotiations. . . . Your attitude for the past four years has been to disregard the union, to avoid compromise at any cost . . . and to continue to suppress the rights of individual players. . . . The players accuse you of taking freedom from the players with no justification. . . . You are guilty of indifference to social changes which have occurred since the early '6os. You have perpetuated an unjust system of control over athletes headed by those who have demonstrated disdain for the constitutional rights of athletes.'

The stage was set; the lines were drawn. The relationship between union and management had turned hostile. Talks stalled (again), then broke off on 26 June. With training camps set to open on 3 July, the union instructed veterans not to report until an agreement was reached. Most of them stayed out until 11 August, when Garvey, watching the strike collapse rapidly, announced plan B: the players would return to work without a contract and take their fight to court. Dues were raised to finance the court battle, and Garvey now had to collect them himself since, without a contract, the union had no automatic collection from players' paychecks. All bets were laid on <u>Mackey vs. NFL</u>. 'We had to win,' Garvey said. 'If we lost Mackey, we were out.'

The trial began in Minneapolis on 3 February 1975. It took 55 days and heard 63 witnesses give more than 12,000 pages of testimony. The decision in favour of the plaintiff came in on 29 December. The League quickly appealed. Though the union had reported losses of $600,000 while pursuing the case, and Ed Garvey had even mortgaged his house, the union now had leverage it hadn't known before. 'Now the men who had risked everything seemed to have won everything,' wrote Harris.

By 1976, the union had a new president, Miami Dolphins defensive back Dick Anderson, who went to great lengths to steer the focus from Ed Garvey to the issues. 'Garvey is our executive director, he works for us. He is still with us, but our policies are set by the elected officers and a seven-man executive council, all players.' Anderson's approach was markedly more conciliatory than Garvey's, and in time, the two were known to be at odds on a number of issues. So, the

League naturally approached and pursued Anderson prior to negotiations for the 1977 agreement. With the Mackey decision hanging over its head, the League, represented by Dan Rooney (who had taken over the Management Council's negotiations) sought a compromise. In return for improvements in pension, minimum salaries, and protection for players' rights, the NFL wanted to preserve its rights of acquisiton and rights of transfer under the Rozelle Rule. The two sides worked out a compensation formula, and by early August had an agreement they felt would be acceptable to the union. But when Anderson presented the agreement to the union's executive committee on 31 August, 'Garvey convinced everyone this was no way to do business,' as one union official said. 'He called them secret agreements. Anderson's proposal was shot down quickly and it would have been voted down no matter what was in it. You can't cut deals without the knowledge of the executive committee. Who knows what's going on? Garvey was right. It's no way to do business.'

When the appeals court hearing the Mackey case announced its decision (18 October 1976) – adding that if the two sides agreed on a compromise to the Rozelle Rule, the arrangement would be exempt from antitrust laws – Garvey felt obliged to negotiate. For over two years the union had been without the income derived from the automatic payroll deduction of membership's monthly dues and membership had dropped dramatically to about 300. The union was coming close to going out of business. In November, it reported net losses of nearly $1 million since 1974. The League therefore concluded that the Rozelle Rule was probably not as important to Garvey as, among other things, a cash settlement of the lawsuits the union had won. So, after almost three months of negotiating, the two sides agreed on a five-year contract shortly before midnight on 16 February 1977. The union gained several concessions, including recognition as a fully fledged National Labour Relations Board union, an agency shop where you have to pay dues even if you don't join. The League also agreed to settle the Mackey case with a $13.65 million payment. 'In return, the National Football League Players' Association accepted the Rozelle Rule, completely abandoning the free agency it had won little more than a year earlier,' wrote David Harris. 'It was the most controversial concession Ed Garvey could have made.' Many observers considered it a sellout.

Garvey's turn-around *was* a huge sellout, but one that he considered worth it. His motives were strictly financial; he lost face, friends, and respect. Indeed, he's fortunate not to have lost most of his teeth. Many players objected when they learned the terms of the agreement. The court had struck down the League's draft system and its Rozelle Rule as illegal. Unrestricted free agency would have benefited many players right away, and an overwhelming majority of them in the long run. Unfortunately, by the time the court decision was reached, Garvey had lost sight of the overall picture, and focused instead on an immediate 'quick fix' for the union's financial woes. Meanwhile, the membership had worked for over two years without a contract (following the 42-day strike), and was applying tremendous pressure on Garvey to obtain a collective bargaining agreement with management. Apparently, *at the time*, the $107 million package of benefits and the $13.65 million settlement of the Mackey case overrode free agency in terms of importance.

Garvey's long-range plan was to accumulate a strike fund from part of the settlement money, to prepare for when the contract expired. They would enter the fight against management well prepared the next time. However, the cash mysteriously disappeared; or perhaps it never accumulated in the first place. There had been poor investments, and expenditures had more than doubled. Whatever the case, when the union prepared for the 1982 negotiations, they did so knowing there was no strike fund for them to fall back on. Garvey was under steadily mounting pressure as negotiations approached. After trading away the rights of free agency won by the Mackey case, he knew he had to deliver in 1982.

He decided to do so by demanding a piece of the football business itself, i.e. 'percentage of the gross'. In lieu of free agency, the union would demand 55 per cent of all teams' gross income. The money, he reasoned, would be worth much more than free agency.

His assistant (and soon to be ex-friend), Bob Moore, thought differently. Though he considered percentage of the gross a good idea, he realised that 'the players didn't like it'. Garvey, he said, 'was in it for the visibility and ego. He was trying to be a senator.' Moore took exception to the way Garvey seemed to be shoving percentage of the gross down the players' throats: 'He was like a fucking used car salesman. . . . He would go to the chalkboard and do the figures. He would estimate teams' costs and percentages. Then he'd say, "Here's what percentage of the gross means." The way he figured it everybody would make three times as much as they were making then. After that, Garvey would ask the players, "What do you think?" Everyone agreed with him. He was amassing an overwhelming majority.

'Things had to come to a head. There were four or five guys on the executive committee who wanted Garvey's ass, who felt we couldn't go on strike with him, and I called them. I told them this was our last chance to dump Garvey before it was too late.'

Moore called Gary Fencik, a defensive back for the Chicago Bears, linebacker Dewey Selmon of the Tampa Bay Buccaneers, Keith Fahnhorst, an offensive tackle for the San Francisco 49ers, and outgoing union president, Washington Redskins centre Len Hauss. They met at Gary Fencik's apartment. Moore continued: 'Garvey got word of what we were up to. We made some serious mistakes. . . . We didn't understand how powerful Garvey was.'

The next day, at the player reps' meeting, Bob Moore resigned his post as the NFLPA's assistant director. Then he launched his argument for dumping Garvey, emphasising what he called poor management of the union, Garvey's lack of respect in the eyes of the players, and that the union could not get a good contract with him at the helm.

The pro-Garvey faction, headed by Oakland Raiders offensive lineman Gene Upshaw, the union's incoming president, presented three arguments for retaining Garvey: (1) the entire union staff of over 40 employees would resign if he were removed from office – 'That scared the shit out of a lot of players,' said Moore; (2) negotiations were about to begin, so it was too late to fire him; and (3) the attack on Garvey was 'racially motivated' (because of his multiracial policies, which some interpreted as pro-black and hence, incredibly, anti-white). The result was that Garvey stayed and Bob Moore's resignation stood. At the end of June 1981, Moore returned to California to finish law school.

When negotiations began on 16 February 1982, Gene Upshaw was the new NFLPA president. He, Garvey, and about 30 others, mostly players, attended the meeting. It was, to say the least, unsuccessful. By the end of the opening session, people were shouting at each other. They met again two days later, and again ended up shouting at each other. The talks, a frustrating series of starts and stops, continued through the summer, but broke off after management's final offer ($1.6 billion over five years towards players' salaries, and $60 million 'money now' giving each veteran $60,000 when the agreement was settled) was rejected by the union, and their counteroffer (drop percentage of the gross for $1.6 billion over four years) was rejected by management.

The strike began on 20 September 1982. It was the first time in its history that an NFL game was cancelled because of an industrial dispute. In the owners' opinion, it was Garvey's strike. Former Philadelphia Eagles owner Leonard Toss ranted, 'Garvey is a horse's ass. He promised the young people in the union the moon and they thought he could deliver. He never gave them the true story.' Garvey, by now used to being maligned by the owners, chose to stay mainly in the background during the strike. Most of the union's statements were made by Upshaw. The new president played a highly visible secondary role to Garvey. Unfortunately for him, the media portrayed him as stubborn, belligerent, and heavy-handed. There was no professional football for 57 days.

Behind the 'united front' that the union presented to the public, the absence of a strike fund was beginning to be felt by the players; support for Garvey was dwindling proportionately. By 12 November, he was feeling somewhat desperate. On 15 November he was back in a negotiating session, this time with the addition of a mutually agreed-upon mediator – Paul Martha. An agreement was reached on 16 November, but it was certainly nothing for Ed Garvey to brag about. It was, in fact, the same offer the owners had made before the strike began.

The membership was angry and bitter. They ratified the contract, but few had good feelings about it. By January 1983, players on several teams had voted to fire Garvey. Instead, he chose to resign. In June, he left the NFLPA to pursue a political career in Wisconsin.

The new executive director was former union president Gene Upshaw. He began immediately to distance himself from the Garvey approach, which had not enhanced his image, nor that of the NFLPA. 'When people think of the National Football League Players' Association, it doesn't rank up there with some of the most credible organisations in the country,' Upshaw said. 'I want our image changed.'

He has worked continuously for that change. Says Mike Davis, a friend and colleague, 'Gene has got a tremendous amount of leadership ability. He encourages questions and participation. And if there's a question he can't answer, he'll bring in the head of department who *can* answer it.

'Gene's whole ambition is for his name to be synonymous with the NFL Players' Association and how they finally arrived. He wants to be able to say, "Well, I was part of the group that finally brought free agency into vogue; I was part of the group that finally brought the pre-'59 players, the past players, the present players, and the future players up to a respectable retirement pension level; I'm the guy who spearheaded that." *That* is his ambition. He doesn't aspire to be a governor.'

Others may disagree with this view; Upshaw's penchant for politics is pretty well known, and though his immediate goal is undoubtedly to strengthen the union, it is probably not his *whole* ambition.

As the most visible union official, Upshaw is constantly attacked by owners and players alike. He led the players in their 1987 work stoppage on the strength of the directives given him by those very players. Yet, when it collapsed, he took the heat. The fact is, the membership, not the leadership failed in '87. Repeatedly, as many as 97 per cent of the players voted to authorise a strike, and stuck by that decision – until the strike began. Then, they had second thoughts; so the strike failed.

Gene Upshaw, however, continued the fight. 'We've tried bargaining, we've been on strike. Now we'll let the courts decide.'

Chapter Four

The first major work stoppage against the National Football League had occurred on 1 July 1974. Still frustrated by what they considered 'failed' negotiations in 1970, the National Football League Players' Association had poised itself in a combative stance as it prepared for the 1974 contract negotiations with the NFL Management Council.

The players' demands were called 'freedom issues', and they presented a list of 58 of them at the opening session on 16 March 1974. With the case of Mackey vs. NFL still awaiting trial, the union's chief demand was elimination of the Rozelle Rule, which would create total free agency, and elimination of the option clause. The option clause allows a player to play out his option, that is, play one season beyond his contract's expiration and then be free to negotiate with other teams. The Rozelle Rule or compensation clause stated, however, that if a player changes teams after his contract is up, his old team must be compensated by his new team with a player of equal calibre. That player would be selected by Commissioner Rozelle. The union considered the rule tantamount to slavery, and management considered it necessary to maintain 'competitive balance'. Former Baltimore Colts tight end John Mackey, the NFLPA president in 1974, wrote in the *New York Times*: 'Players demand freedom. They demand the rights of citizenship. They demand the constitutional protections afforded all other citizens of this country. Pete Rozelle and [NFL lawyer] Ted Kheel will answer that athletes are "well paid" for giving up their freedom, that the system would not survive if athletes were free to negotiate with more than one employer. I am appalled that in the United States of America, people can still make economic arguments to justify the taking away of a man's freedom and dignity. . . . You cannot pay me enough for me to allow you to sell me or trade me. I was born in a society dedicated to freedom. . . . Some say that freedom for athletes will destroy the NFL. I say nonsense. Freedom will

27

allow the NFL to flourish. But I also say this: If freedom will destroy the NFL, then the NFL should be destroyed. Then a new and better League run by those who understand free enterprise, based upon the freedom of the players, would take its place. Our society cannot tolerate a system that allows self-appointed barons with their highly paid lawyers to deprive any segment of our society of its freedom.'

Ted Kheel, representing management, countered: 'This system has worked reasonably well. The players' demand for "no system" would constitute anarchy.' On the economic issues, he continued, '. . . the union wants to retain bargaining rights on the same money matters over which the union has waived bargaining rights. Thus, for example, it has called for a bonus of "not less than" $2,500 to each traded player above moving expenses, of "not less than" $25,000 for each player on the victorious Super Bowl team, of "not less than" stated amounts for the playoff games. . . . It seeks to recapture bargaining rights on money matters the players will later be negotiating individually. . . . Does the union really mean to force the owners to bargain twice on the same money matters?'

The union submitted 33 additional demands in May, bringing the total to 90. Negotiations broke off on 26 June. On 1 July veteran players were ordered not to report to training camps, scheduled to open on 3 July, until an agreement was reached. The strike was on.

It had a 'deep personal impact' on New York Giants owner Wellington Mara, who was also chairman of the NFL Management Council's executive committee. 'I never really believed it would happen,' he said. 'It was a bolt out of the blue to realise players had grievances.'

The two sides met on 12 July, and again on 18 July. Both times, they rejected each other's proposals, and left the bargaining table. On 29 July they met again, this time with a federal mediator. Again, no progress was made, and the mediator called for a five-day recess. With exhibition games scheduled to begin on 2 August, NFLPA president Bill Curry was asked if players might report to training camp while contract negotiations continued. 'We'd have to make a decision on that at the time, but my feeling is that we ought to go ahead and sign an agreement before reporting. We went to camp without a contract in 1970 and we ran into some problems that were hard to solve because we didn't have a contract. Then it took us almost a year to get a contract.'

Meanwhile the union's resolve and the strike were crumbling rapidly. On 7 August, after 38 days on strike, the League reported that 360 veteran players had crossed picket lines. Management intensified its pressure by attacking the union's foundation: its 26 player representatives. 'Ken Reeves, Atlanta's player rep, was walking a picket line when Falcons owner Rankin Smith drove up in a car with the team's coach and told Reeves to take his picket sign to New Orleans because he'd been traded. The union's president, first vice-president, and second vice-president would either be dropped or traded as well.

Management, said Ed Garvey, 'smelled blood'. After five days back at the negotiating table, they threatened to walk out for good unless the 'freedom issues' were dropped completely. Additionally, they wanted the union to drop Mackey vs. NFL. When the union refused, management walked out. The players had lost. Garvey now went to Plan B, which was to return to work without a contract and continue their battle in court with Mackey vs. NFL. On 11 August, on the recommendation of federal mediator William J. Usery Jr, Garvey announced that union members would be asked to report to training camps on 13 August, so that a 14-day 'cooling-off period' could take place prior to resuming productive talks. The decision was not unanimous among the player representatives or the union's executive committee. 'They knew when they went back they would be dropped,' explained Garvey. Indeed, union casualties were high: within a year, a total of 20 union officers and player reps had been dropped or traded. Of the seven men on the union's negotiating committee, only two still had jobs a year after they set up their first picket line. On Wellington Mara's Giants, almost every player who had stayed out during the strike was gone within a month.

The strike also took its toll on the fans. Unfortunately for the union, however, management's clever manipulation of the media resulted in the fans' sentiment and sympathy favouring the owners, not the players. In separate polls taken by the *Milwaukee Journal* in Wisconsin, and by radio station WTAG in Worcester, Massachusetts, an overwhelming majority of the respondents (as much as 88 per cent) agreed with the owners' position. Many added that they would do without NFL football for a year if it would help the owners keep the players from gaining 'unrealistic concessions that would be damaging to pro football'.

But the late, great Red Smith, renowned sportswriter for the *New York Times*, said that the perceptions of the public, and also of some sportswriters, may have been somewhat distorted; he explained why. The *Boston Globe* had printed an editorial on 6 August which read in part: 'While the parties to the dispute are making speeches about freedom and the future of the game, it is the fans who are bearing and will continue to bear the brunt of this foolishness.' Red took exception to that and wrote in his column the next day:

There may be some in the audience who do not scorn freedom as foolishness or regard a minimum salary of $13,000 as 'enough fame, fortune and financial security' to buy off human dignity. In fairness to the men who shape the *Globe*'s editorial policy, it should be remembered that perhaps those passing judgment on the case did so with information that was incomplete and in some cases erroneous. This, we are assured on excellent authority, has been known to happen.

For instance, the statement that it is the fans who bear the brunt of the foolishness is, to use an expression current in high places, 'at variance' with the facts. Over the weekend more than a quarter-million fans put their ticket money back in their pockets, and when the owners toted up receipts from exhibition games, about $2 million worth of brunt caught them in the eye.

At the same time, Nielsen ratings of the exhibitions dropped off dramatically, making it clear that the customers are not going to pay $7 or $8 a pop to watch rookies and retreads, and indeed, won't even tune them in on free television. The lesson for club owners and TV sponsors was enunciated years ago by an uncommonly wise man. The quotation usually begins, 'You may fool all of the people some of the time,' but actually the passage starts with a warning: 'If you once forfeit the confidence of your fellow citizens, you can never regain their respect and esteem.'

Striking players complain that they have been ill-used by

the press, which seldom makes a conscientious effort to present their side of the dispute. It is a valid complaint, though it is not a case of reporters being bought off for a cold hotdog and presweetened coffee between halves.

A sportswriter is often a fan sun-blinded by his enthusiasm. He regards the game as more important than the human beings who play it. He accepts the status quo because that is the only status he is familiar with and because the Establishment tells him it is essential to the 'survival of the game as we know it'. He buys that hogwash because in most cases it is the owner, coach and press agent who have his ear, not the players.

The daily headlines announcing the deflection of this or that established player from the picket lines offer an example of the use the League is making of its public relations force. . . . League announcements do not mention that three-fourths of the membership of the Players' Association are still out, that some have reported and then walked out, that not quite enough 'regulars' to staff three of the 26 teams are in camp. . . . [Sounds like 1987?]

So, after 42 days on strike, the players returned to work without a contract for the 14-day 'cooling-off' period. That 14 turned into 14 more, and then 14 more. When training camps opened in 1975, the contract negotiations were still dragging on, and Ed Garvey was still unable to maintain a united front among the players.

On 13 September 1975, the Saturday before their final exhibition game against the New York Jets, the New England Patriots voted 39–2 to stage a wildcat strike of their own, and refuse to play that game. The League took immediate action in response to the strike vote and issued the following statement: 'If the game is not played as scheduled, the players will not be paid, nor can they practise until a collective bargaining agreement is signed or a no-strike pledge given by the union.'

On Sunday, the New York Giants voted to delay the start of their game against the Miami Dolphins for a half-hour in a show of sympathy for the Patriots. But after a pregame locker-room visit by Miami coach Don Shula and four Dolphin co-captains, they reversed their decision and the game started eight minutes late. Several other clubs held meetings to decide what action, if any, to take. There were rumours that the St Louis Cardinals would join the strike and refuse to play the Denver Broncos. They proved to be untrue, and the game went on. But by Wednesday, 17 September, the New York Jets, Washington Redskins, New York Giants and Detroit Lions had joined the Patriots on strike. Still, there was no unanimity among the team. Five were on strike, three were not on strike, seven were undecided, and eleven had no opinion.

A settlement meeting was called at the New York offices of the NFL Management Council on Wednesday evening. The key people – Federal Mediator William J. Usery, Garvey and Sargent Karch, executive director of the Management Council – were joined by four players: offensive lineman Doug Van Horn and Dick Enderle of the Giants, defensive lineman Richard Neal of the Jets, and defensive back Dick Anderson of the Dolphins. The negotiations got intense around midnight, and ended at 9 a.m. Thursday morning with an agreement to stop the strike and open the regular season as scheduled on Sunday, 21 September. The key to the truce was a promise by the owners to present a substantial contract offer by Monday, 22 September.

The issues in the 1974 dispute were finally settled on 29 December 1975. Federal judge Earl R. Larson ruled, in the case of John Mackey et al vs. National Football League, that the Rozelle Rule was in violation of antitrust laws, and was therefore illegal. On 18 October 1976, the decision was upheld in the appeals court, but the appellate judge also ruled that should the two sides negotiate and agree upon the Rozelle Rule in collective bargaining, it would then be exempt from antitrust law.

By the time the Mackey decision came in, the union had reported substantial financial losses, and Ed Garvey was being pressured from all sides for an agreement. Ironically, management knew it had the upper hand, and that in return for a cash settlement, Garvey would most likely negotiate a compromise to the Rozelle Rule. They were right.

On 16 February 1977, a five-year contract was agreed on by both sides. The total cost of the agreement was estimated at $107 million. In return for completely abandoning the free agency the players had won in the Mackey case, and accepting the same Rozelle Rule that it had been fighting for the past three years – thereby making an illegal system legal – the union gained several concessions from management. Among them: increases in minimum salaries, preseason and postseason pay; improved insurance, medical and dental benefits; contributions totalling more than $55 million to the pension plan; and a $13.65 million damage settlement from the Mackey case, to be distributed among 3,200 active and former players. The controversial union concession ended the longest industrial dispute in football business history, and was described as 'the biggest sellout by a union in sports history'.

Over the five-year life of the 1977 agreement, the union should have been, theoretically, more financially secure than ever before. It had received a payment of $750,000 as part of the settlement of the Mackey case and of a related case, <u>Alexander vs. NFL</u>, and had regained automatic dues collection from players' paychecks, raising its net assets from minus $233,000 to plus $608,000 in one year. Ed Garvey received a 100 per cent salary increase, and was repaid the money he had borrowed against his house. His long-range plan had been to use the settlement money to form a strike fund in preparation for the upcoming contract talks. Yet, the union's coffers were mysteriously vacuous.

It seems that by the end of 1977, Garvey (apparently satisfied with his football 'accomplishments') had turned his attention to organising other sports. According to Bob Moore, a former NFLPA vice-president, and ex-friend of Garvey, 'Ed envisaged himself being a big man in the AFL–CIO (the American Federation of Labour/Congress of Industrial Organisations – two bodies which merged several years ago to form the largest, most powerful union in the country). He thought athletes' notoriety could make them a major industrial force. He envisaged a Federation of Professional Athletes that would include all sports, with himself as its head. . . . The biggest problem was that the union leaders in baseball, basketball, and hockey all hated Garvey, so that part never got off the ground. In the meantime, he went after the unorganised sports.' Soccer was his main target; his new union would be called the North American Soccer League Players' Association. To get started, his NASLPA received a $500,000 loan from his NFLPA. It was a shrewd move – the investment was a perfectly legal one, but the venture soon collapsed in a sea of red ink, and by 1981 all of Garvey's energies were once again directed towards the NFL. By then, his problems were immediate and serious. Pressure was mounting from all sides as the '82 negotiations approached. There was no strike fund; he was still being criticised for trading away the free agency won in the Mackey case; and the players' average pay was still the lowest of America's three major professional sports. There had been scattered attempts since 1977 to oust him from his post. The heat was on and Ed Garvey knew it.

His answer to the problems proved in the end to be his undoing. But at the time, 'percentage of the gross' seemed to be the most logical conclusion. Free agency, Garvey reasoned, was a dead issue. A much more valuable arrangement would be one in which the players owned part of the business itself. The union, therefore, would demand that 55 per cent of all teams' gross income should go towards players' salaries, to be distributed by the union according to position and seniority. He then set out on a campaign to sell the idea to the membership. And he was extremely successful – at first.

His first and most important selling point was the gross underpayment of football players, as compared to baseball and basketball players. Though the revenues generated by the three sports varied only slightly, the average salaries of NFL players fell more than 150 per cent below those of baseball and basketball players. To illustrate his point, Garvey cited the recent signing of baseball player George Foster by the New York Mets for over $1 million per year, plus bonuses. 'I reviewed the contracts for the [Super Bowl participants] Bengal and 49er players at the [so-called] 'skill positions' for 1981, and included pay for the Super Bowl game. At quarterback we had Joe Mantana and Ken Anderson. The running backs were Pete Johnson, Charles Alexander, Ricky Patton and Earl Cooper; at wide receiver were Issac Curtis, Cris Collinsworth, Freddie Solomon, and Dwight Clark; and at tight end, Dan Ross and Charlie Young. Taking George Foster's salary plus his bonus payments and applying it to these 12 players, we could pay their annual salaries, bonuses for 1981 and Super Bowl pay, and still have plenty to pay the 1982 salaries of Forrest Gregg and Bill Walsh, the coaches.'

34

But Foster was a superstar. What about the average player? In 1981, basketball's average salary was $215,000; baseball's was $192,000; football's was $90,000. That should put the salary structure of the three sports into some perspective. Consider, also, that the NFL was the number one revenue-producing league in the country, grossing several hundred million dollars per year. Garvey argued that the players would be better served being paid from a union-controlled fund, based on position and seniority, with significant bonuses for outstanding performance and postseason play, than from individually negotiated wages. Careers would be extended, he continued, because owners would no longer have an economic reason for dropping a veteran in favour of a less talented, but less expensive rookie (first-year player). 'Fair pay and longer careers. That's worth a fight.' The players bought it, hook, line, and sinker.

Management, on the other hand, was adamant. Naturally, they resented the threat of a strike being linked to the union's demands. Money was the central issue, and they were willing to cough up more money. But it got to be a personal thing against Garvey. If a strike happened, they would consider it Garvey's strike. He was trying to 'wrest the decision-making power from the owners', and they would have none of it! Said Jack Donlan, executive director of the NFL Management Council, 'The two sides can negotiate money, but they cannot negotiate philosophy. Even a strike will not alter philosophy. If management opposes a percentage of the gross concept before a walkout, it will continue to oppose it even when the action ends. . . . That and the fact that the Players' Association has had considerable difficulty managing its own business are reasons enough why we will not invite them to help us run ours.'

The next two months were filled with starts and stops; meetings and no progress; charges and counter charges. On 13 April the union broke off the talks and filed a complaint with the National Labour Relations Board charging the League with unfair industrial practice. They cited a telephone poll being conducted by the *Kansas City Times*, and accused management of providing the newspaper with the players' home telephone numbers and of jointly conducting the survey concerning players' union activities and willingness to strike.

Additionally, Gene Upshaw, NFLPA president, said the Management Council had not submitted requested information regarding television contracts and other team data.

Donlan said it was a smoke-screen: 'They just put their coats on and walked out. They keep bringing up side issues like this poll. I don't think they want to negotiate. All I hear is strike.'

On 8 June an eight-hour session ended with neither side speaking to the other for the last hour. 'I think the union has a clear and unequivocal understanding: we are not going to buy today, in July, in September, or 100 days into a strike a percentage of the gross,' said Donlan.

With the 15 July expiration date just 60 hours away, the Management Council presented a five-year contract proposal at the noon session on 13 July. The union flatly rejected it and the meeting turned into a shouting match.

Two weeks before the first exhibition game was scheduled, Donlan threatened a lockout if an agreement were not reached by the time the regular season began. He said the owners did not want to put money in the players' pockets so that they could ride out a strike.

Meanwhile, the players were beginning to argue among themselves. A few said they would not support or honour a strike, but by the time the exhibition season began, they appeared unified and very solid in their resolve. The Washington Redskins and the Miami Dolphins agreed to defy the League's rule against 'fraternisation with opponents' and shake hands on the field before the start of their game. 'The handshake will not be disruptive, and it will take less than one minute,' said Redskins player representative Mark Murphy. 'We voted unanimously in a team meeting that we want to make a collective action to show we are solid.' In nine of the ten exhibition games on Saturday, 14 August, the teams exchanged handshakes at midfield before kickoff. (The Los Angeles Rams and Denver Broncos were the only teams not participating.) What became known as the 'solidarity handshake' took place before each game prior to the strike. The reactions to it varied. The League threatened to fine players who shook hands a minimum of $100 (the Seattle Seahawks were fined *one half* of their game checks); then backed off the next weekend in a 'conciliatory' gesture aimed at getting the union back to the bargaining table. Many of the fans booed the handshake.

Early in September, the owners upped the stakes of their $1.6 billion, five-year proposal by offering bonuses ('now money') of as much as $60,000 per player. But the union rejected it, and added that at least one team, the Seattle Seahawks, might boycott their 12 September game (the regular season opener) because their player representative, Sam McCullum, had been dropped. By then, player reps from several teams, including the New Orleans Saints, Buffalo Bills and Baltimore Colts, were getting the axe, though management insisted that their union activities were not a factor. The owners were becoming increasingly frustrated with the unproductive bargaining sessions, and by 9 September had begun to seriously consider a lockout. Then, on Thursday, 16 September, Ed Garvey announced that unless the owners got serious about bargaining, a strike would begin on Tuesday, 21 September. Though the union had originally planned to wait until the third week of games had passed, Garvey said that management's failure to bargain seriously 'forced us to go out earlier than we wanted to'. At the same time, management was just about fed up. Jack Donlan responded to the projected strike date: 'This is entirely consistent with the union's game plan from the beginning. . . . They refused to make counterproposals. They've refused mediation. And they've rejected our proposals out of hand. The whole thing has been a charade. I will tell the union that if they are not prepared to make a full, complete counterproposal there is no sense in meeting again.'

With the strike a near certainty, the owners now began to examine their options. They would try to field teams even if a strike was called. Using free agents, rookies, and any veterans crossing picket lines, they would make up their numbers and continue games. (Sounds like 1987, huh?)

Friday, 17 September was the last time the two sides met before the strike of 1982. The union submitted a surprise proposal which dropped its demand for 55 per cent of the gross revenues (which, according to Upshaw, had been 'etched in stone') in favour of 50 per cent of the television revenue for 1982 through 1985. Basically, they were asking for the same $1.6 billion that management had offered over five years, but they wanted it apportioned over four years. The owners rejected the offer, talks were suspended with no future negotiations scheduled, and a work stoppage, barring any un-foreseen developments, was now inevitable.

The strike officially began on the evening of 20 September, immediately following the nationally televised 'Monday Night Football' game between the New York Giants and the Green Bay Packers (which the Packers won, 27–19). After a two and a half hour meeting of the union's executive committee in midtown New York, Upshaw made the announcement at a news conference: 'The impassse has left us no choice but to use the only weapon we have to force management to bargain with us. At the conclusion of tonight's game between the New York Giants and the Green Bay Packers, all NFL training facilities will be struck. There will be no practices, no workouts or training. No games will be played until management abandons its unlawful course, engages in collective bargain-ing and executes a fair and equitable agreement.'

Less than one hour later, the NFL Management Council responded: 'We have not been informed officially of the union's actions, but we are aware of the press conference today. We regret the union has chosen this path. . . . We will proceed with our scheduled executive committee meeting tonight and determine our course of action. After we have informed the member clubs of our decisions and what actions we should take, we will explain our position to the public.'

The impact was immediate and wide-ranging. From the players and the owners to the parking lot attendants and con-cessionaires; from the highest levels of American banking to the neighbourhood bookmaker, thousands of people whose work depended on football were threatened by the strike.

Support by the players was strong, if not absolute. Many of them went on strike grudgingly. 'I don't want to strike. That's as simple as I can make it,' said quarterback Jim Zorn of the Seattle Seahawks. 'But I feel obliged to stay out along with the other players.' In Los Angeles, Rams tight end Mike Barber said, 'I'm against what the players are going for.' And defensive back Ricky Woods, a rookie with the Pittsburgh Steel-ers lamented, 'All my life I've worked for this opportunity. Now they're striking on me. . . . I wish I didn't have to make a decision.' That sentiment was echoed among many rookies; naive, perhaps, about the football *business*; anxious just to get on with the football *game*, and make their marks on the NFL.

Said Mike Pagel, a rookie quarterback for the (then) Baltimore Colts: 'I understand the issues pretty well, and I know the players have a point and management has its point, but what I want to do right now is play football. I really don't want a strike. Me and the other young guys on the team are actually just starting to learn how this game is played.' But overall, the players presented a united front. They spoke of solidarity and of the union's ability to withstand a lengthy strike. Washington Redskins player rep Mark Murphy warned, 'The owners have made a big mistake. They have greatly underestimated the union's strength. The players are very unified. Management's attempts to divide us have made us stronger.'

The owners tried for almost a year to get strike insurance, but were unable to because of the 50-day strike by major League baseball players in 1981. Instead, they arranged for $150 million credit from a consortium of banks, which any club could borrow against as needed 'for operating expenses'. But the union, remember, had no strike fund. Nor did the countless other people whose jobs were a part of every football game. The stadium security guards, maintenance crews, hot dog vendors and ticket sellers were all thrown out of work. In New York alone, the city stood to lose over $100,000 each time a game in its stadium was cancelled. Rent, sales tax, and revenue from fans using public transport accounted for over $60,000 per game.

Likewise, the three television networks had to make some financial adjustments to the $2.2 billion contract the League had recently signed. CBS had paid close to $750 million for the five-year arrangement; ABC had paid almost $700 million, and NBC had paid about $650 million.

Ed Garvey, meanwhile, was still considered by many to be the primary villain. Sportswriter Dave Anderson said in his *New York Times* column: 'The suspicion is that Ed Garvey has provoked a strike in order to project himself on an ego trip into politics someday. For the duration of the strike, Ed Garvey at last will have upstaged Pete Rozelle as pro football's most important individual who doesn't wear a helmet or a headset. For the first time, the executive director of the NFL Players' Association is now a national newsmaker, followed by reporters and cameras as if he had accomplished something truly important in American history instead of merely stopping the NFL schedule.'

For the players and coaches, the first few days of the strike were quiet; dismal; even eerie. Most coaches continued with their usual routine of reviewing game films, and preparing game plans for their next (scheduled) opponent. 'We keep going. If something breaks we want to be prepared,' said Jets head coach Walt Michaels. But the locker rooms were silent, like a ghost-town, on Day One. When players returned to gather their belongings, some of them were surprised to find their lockers stripped and their belongings stored away. They had been locked out. 'They're serious about this, aren't they?' said Jeff Weston, a lineman for the New York Giants. The players arranged to meet away from their stadiums to organise team workouts; they were not allowed to do so on any NFL facility.

While management realised rather quickly that fielding non-union teams of NFL calibre was a very unlikely venture, the union talk soon turned to organising a six-team 'All-Star League' composed of striking players. The league would begin play on 10 October and cable network TBS – the Turner Broadcasting System – announced its plans to televise the games. Management warned that it would take legal action against any player who joined the union league, based on a clause in every player's contract prohibiting participation in any non-NFL football-related activity that involves risk of personal injury. Union counsel Dick Berthelsen countered by arguing the validity of the standard players' contract, which was 'unilaterally imposed upon the players by the clubs in 1976, before there was a collective bargaining agreement in 1977'. Still, five courts granted temporary restraining orders to NFL clubs trying to keep their players out of the union-sponsored games. The first two games were a monumental flop anyway, and the remaining ones were soon cancelled.

And what about the American football fan? Well, we began to feel the full impact of the walkout on the first Sunday without the usual fare of televised professional games. We desperately sought other diversions. People took long walks, cleaned their yards, washed their cars, played golf, or went shopping. The baseball playoffs and the World Series were coming up. There was college football, Canadian football, the start of the National Hockey League season, and the National Basketball Association season. 'But for the National Football League fan, as in fanatic,' wrote Dave Anderson, 'there is no substitute. Not reruns of memorable games, not Canadian Football League games. To the NFL's devoted followers, Sunday afternoon means NFL football. Nothing less. And nothing else.' One college football player said he felt deprived. 'It's depressing missing a part of your weekly routine. Normally, I come from church and have lunch, then watch football for most of the afternoon. . . . Both the owners and the players are hurting the public, which pays the salaries. I think they are both stupid.' But the fans wouldn't go very far away. Everybody knew it. Most fans didn't really understand the details of the dispute, and really didn't want to. Most fans wouldn't care about the details of any new collective bargaining agreement. All most fans were interested in was when the season would resume, and what the odds would be.

The negotiations dragged on. With each side blaming the other, they would start, and stop, and start again, and stop again. A secret meeting was arranged in early October by two Harvard University professors. Roger Fisher, who taught mediation, negotiation and dispute resolution, and Paul Weiler, who taught industrial law, scheduled a meeting in Boston between the chief negotiators for the League and for the union. But Garvey said he was not informed in time for any union representatives to accept, and the meeting was cancelled.

On 12 October a new private mediator, 73-year-old Sam Kagel, entered the negotiations. The highly regarded arbitrator immediately announced a news blackout as a condition of his mediation. There was guarded optimism on both sides. The first reports of progress came on 14 October, as the two sides worked out some of the 'lesser things' such as grievance procedures, minicamps, and players' access to their personal and medical records. The biggest issue – the means by which the players would be paid, union wage-scale or individual negotiations – remained unresolved.

On 23 October Mr Kagel called for an indefinite recess of negotiations so that both sides could 're-examine and reassess their respective positions on the economic issues'.

As the strike wore on, Garvey was having increasing difficulty in keeping the membership united. The absence of a strike fund was being felt more and more. Russ Francis, a tight end for the San Francisco 49ers, called for a secret ballot to determine whether the players were ready to return to work without a contract while negotiations continued. The pressures on Garvey were mounting.

On 4 November management made its 'best offer': $1.3 billion over four years, plus the 'now money' bonuses offered earlier. Garvey, by now beaten and searching for something to save his face, asked for a 'formal gesture' to establish the union's right to negotiate wages. Management refused, negotiations broke off, and on 6 November Mr Kagel withdrew his services and flew home to San Francisco.

The union membership was about to cave in. They'd been out of work for over 50 days. Players on four teams voted by overwhelming margins to accept the owners' offer and return to work. On 12 November, in a state of desperation, Garvey contacted Dan Rooney, a member of the Management Council's executive committee. The two of them, now certain that the season was shot to hell, racked their brains for a solution; or at least for someone to mediate. They agreed on Paul Martha, a 39-year-old Pittsburgh lawyer.

Martha was vice-president and general counsel of the San Francisco 49ers, the Pittsburgh Penguins of the National Hockey League, and the Pittsburgh Spirit of the (now defunct) Major Indoor Soccer League. An ex-player (defensive back/running back for the Pittsburgh Steelers from 1964 through 1969), he was very highly respected on both sides of the dispute. He entered the negotiations as an intermediary on 13 November. He brought the two sides together at the St Regis Hotel in New York, and after two days of meetings, an agreement was announced on Tuesday, 16 November. No one was elated, but almost everyone was relieved. After forcing us (the fans) to suffer through 57 days with no professional football, the union accepted a proposal from management – $1.6 billion over five years – that had been on the table before the strike began. The NFLPA player representatives were not happy. They voted 19–6 to put the agreement to a membership vote, but only three recommended accepting it. 'The strike was a complete failure,' said one player rep. The rank and file was fed up, and ready to go back to work. They ratified the agreement by a margin of 3–1.

The players, the owners, the football stadiums, and all of

the NFL cities were big losers after the strike of '82. The players returned to work angry and bitter after losing over $72 million in wages. There would surely be bad feeling between players and management to contend with. The players felt they had been forced to eat dirt. The owners had won the battle, but had paid dearly for it. Their reported losses totalled over $240 million. The concessionaires and other stadium personnel had lost $22 million. The cities had lost $110 million in overall business, and another $11 million in sales, taxes and rent.

But the fans had lost out too, and they were to lose the owners more money because of it. Before the strike began on 21 September, they had a reputation for remarkable loyalty. But after the strike, some fans were a bit slow to return to the fold. The stadiums would eventually be filled again, but not right away. Fans had found other things to do. And when they did return, there would be booing like the players had never heard before. In the *New York Times* Dave Anderson wrote: 'Every man in the stands who had to stay home and paint the storm windows or accompany his wife to the shopping centre on Sundays is going to take it out on the players. Every fan who had to find something else to do on Monday nights is going to take it out on the players.' The most common reaction, in fact, was 'It's finally over, so to hell with them for a while.'

The schedule of NFL games was revised to complete the season. There would be seven regular season games, which, with the two played before the strike, made a total of nine instead of the usual 16. Three weekends of playoffs would follow, with the Super Bowl being played as scheduled on 30 January.

The Washington Redskins, who had remained united as a team throughout the dispute, came out on top of the heap in the strike-shortened 1982 season. They earned their first play-off spot (the equivalent in British football of a cup tie) in six years with a record of eight wins and one loss, then rolled through the postseason (in which only teams that have qualified for playoffs participate) with impressive victories over the Detroit Lions (31–7), the Minnesota Vikings (21–7), and the Dallas Cowboys (31–17). They defeated the Miami Dolphins, 27–17, to win Super Bowl XVII.

Ed Garvey's days as NFLPA executive director were now numbered. In January 1983, players on several teams voted to fire him. By early February, he saw the handwriting on the wall; he knew he was finished. But he wanted to resign, not be forced out. Amazingly, the union membership allowed him to do so. In June, he made his resignation official and left Washington to pursue a political career in Wisconsin. He ran for the Wisconsin State Senate immediately after leaving the NFPLA, but lost decisively, then faded from public view. He left behind him what David Harris called a 'landmark of financial devastation', and soon became known around NFPLA circles as 'that bastard'.

Chapter Five

Up to the very moment that it happened, I didn't believe that there would be another National Football League players' strike. How could the lessons of 1974 and 1982 be so foolishly ignored? Both sides had a great deal to lose, but I thought the odds were overwhelmingly against the players from the onset. The eventual outcome of a strike seemed painfully obvious; its predictability exceeded only by its injustice.

Negotiations for the 1987 Collective Bargaining Agreement between management and the players of the National Football League began on 20 April 1986. Between 20 April and the 31 August expiry date of the previous contract, the two sides met 17 times, but made little progress. The issues were:

- **Guaranteed contracts** Fewer than five per cent of the NFL players have a guaranteed contract. If a player is dropped (even after an injury), he usually receives very little severance pay. The players wanted their contracts paid to completion.
- **Improvements in the players' pension plan** In the 1982 Collective Bargaining Agreement, the NFL owners committed to contribute $12.5 million per year over five years ($62.5 million) to the players' pension fund. The players charged that the owners still owed $18 million to the pension fund from that commitment, and took the dispute to federal court. Meanwhile, the owners called for no improvements in pension benefits for seasons prior to 1987.

Additionally, the union wanted the players to be vested in the League's pension plan after one season. Currently, a player has to complete four seasons.

- **Free agency** In another attempt at eliminating the Rozelle Rule, the union asked for uncompensated free agency after a player's fourth season in the League. The owners offered to lower but not eliminate (never!) the compensation paid by teams who sign other teams' free agents, with the players' original club retaining the right of first refusal. This was the issue that management held up to the media and the American

45

public as the lynchpin of the players' demands (like percentage of the gross in 1982). This, according to management, was what would make or break the negotiations.

● **Protection for player reps and NFPLA officers from management harassment and discrimination or discharge** During the 1982 strike, many union members, particularly officers and player representatives, were dropped or traded from their teams. In 1987 the practice continued. As the '87 strike was getting into full swing, union vice-president Brian Holloway, an offensive lineman for the New England Patriots, appeared on ABC Television in debate with management representative Jack Donlan. Less than 12 hours later, Holloway was traded to the Los Angeles Raiders. He was one of many union activists to be 'forced out'.

The union also continues its efforts to have pre-1959 players included in the pension fund, where they will be eligible for widows' and survivors' benefits and disability payments.

● **Improvements in other benefits and player rights** One of the major points in this category was the wage scale. The union wanted the minimum salaries raised from the current $50,000 to $90,000 for first-year players, and from $60,000 to $110,000 for second-year players. The owners proposed flat salaries of $60,000 for first-year players, and $70,000 for second-year players. Also included here were roster size (the number of players, both regular and reserve, in training), severance pay, and pay for offseason workouts and mini-camps.

● **Improvement of existing chemical dependency prevention programme** Currently, players took one mandatory drug test in their preseason physical examination, with provisions for further testing if there was reasonable cause. The union proposed a programme which provided for treatment and disciplinary action for drug abuse, but opposed the random testing that management sought.

● **Faster, more effective grievance arbitration** The players felt that disputes with management were not resolved in a timely manner, sometimes taking years to settle.

● **Shorter term for the collective bargaining agreement** This was the only priority of the eight that management and the union reached agreement on (for a while, anyway). The duration of the agreement would be three years. Management later changed its position and proposed a seven-year contract.

The negotiating process – that is, that side seen by the American public, could be compared to the 1983 Heavyweight Championship fight between Larry Holmes and Marvis Frazier. It wasn't even close. The older, eminently more experienced Holmes completely dominated the infant Frazier. It took him less than one round to pummel Frazier into the ground. It got so bad that Holmes himself summoned the referee over to stop the fight. You had to feel for Marvis; even hope for a split second that he'd somehow, miraculously, triumph over all odds. But despite all the prefight hoopla, all the statistically backed possibilities, one knew that power and experience would ultimately prevail. Such was the case when the NFL Players' Association took on the NFL owners.

I could never quite understand why the players took the approach they did. They clearly underestimated just what they were up against. The owners may compete on the playing field, but they are partners in the boardroom, and they presented a truly united front that effectively crushed the strike, and crippled the union in the process. Lest we forget, this team of owners includes some of the wealthiest and shrewdest businessmen in the country. Seven NFL owners are on the *Forbes* magazine's 1987 list of America's richest individuals: Washington Redskins' owner Jack Kent Cooke, San Francisco 49ers' owner Edward J. DeBartolo, Detroit Lions' owner William Clay Ford, New York Jets' owner Leon Hess, Dallas Cowboys' owner H. R. (Bum) Bright, San Diego Chargers' owner Alex Spanos, and Tampa Bay Buccaneers' owner Hugh Culverhouse. The top three (Cooke, DeBartolo, and Ford) have a net worth of more than $1 billion each. Knowing this (and if I knew it, surely they knew it), why did they stage a work stoppage against which the owners had already mounted a defense? And why strike after week three? Why not later in the season when there was more at stake? NFPLA executive committee member Mike Davis, a former Oakland/Los Angeles Raider now with the San Diego Chargers, explained: 'I think we had a real good plan going into this battle. But we had to have the support of the players. Without the players' support, nothing would have worked no matter when we did it. If we'd had every NFL player respecting and recognising what we're trying to do as a union, we would have won significant improvements on all eight of our priorities.

'We went into the bargaining sessions prepared. We had an explanation for anything that we put up on the table for discussion. Mick Luckhurst [kicker, Atlanta Falcons], Mike Kenn [offensive tackle, Atlanta Falcons], George Martin [defensive end, New York Giants], Michael Jackson [line-backer, Seattle Seahawks], James Lofton [receiver, L.A. Raiders], Dan Marino [quarterback, Miami Dolphins], and myself – we had our act together! We had arguments for everything; we had arguments to substantiate the arguments; we had substantiations to substantiate the substantiations! We left no stone unturned, because we knew what we were getting into. We had a membership to represent; not only that, we had ourselves to represent. We had to be right. We had to have our facts. And that's what we went in with.'

Gene Upshaw, former Oakland/L.A. Raider, former NFPLA president, was now the union's executive director and chief negotiator. He, attorney Dick Berthelsen, assistant executive director Doug Allen, and the executive committee comprised the union's negotiating team.

During contract talks in 1982, when he was the union's president, Upshaw had come across as heavy-handed, radical, and belligerent. When the 1987 talks began, he was still haunted by that image. He knew that the way he handled the current negotiations and how the public perceived him would have a tremendous impact on his future. And it is well known that he has nurtured political dreams for a very long time. When he was a Raider, his teammates called him 'The Governor'.

There were many, many negotiating sessions, in several cities: Washington, San Francisco, Philadelphia, New York, Miami, Chicago. Initially, the Management Council was represented by attorney Sargent Karch, former Atlanta Falcons general manager Eddie LeBaron, Management Council executive director Jack Donlan, and John Jones, Donlan's assistant. But the union insisted that ownership should be represented, and soon they were joined by Dan Rooney of the Pittsburgh Steelers and Tex Schramm of the Dallas Cowboys.

Mike Davis described a typical bargaining session: 'First, we'd have breakfast – and no matter *where* we had breakfast, they were somewhere near. We would see them, and pleasantries would be exchanged in passing. We would have our

48

agenda; what we wanted to discuss, at what length, and where we wanted to go with it. And of course, they had theirs. So we'd go to the meeting room and sit down. It was the typical seating arrangement – us against them. But sometimes we'd position ourselves on their side and close to them, so that it looked like we had them surrounded on all sides. It was interesting seeing their reactions. . . . It was almost comical. It was serious, but it was almost comical how they kept us on free agency. Even though we moved to the other issues and discussed all eight points, what they came back with were cutbacks in all eight areas. And when we came out of the bargaining session, they told the press: 'Well, all we did was discuss free agency, and there's no movement.' That was all they wanted to discuss: free agency and how it would destroy football.

'The NFL is the number one spectator sport in America; possibly in the world for all I know. Whenever there's a big game – the AFC and NFC Championship games, or the Super Bowl – all seven continents are plugged in. And the owners are saying that if there were free agency – an open market – in football, it would destroy the system, simply because you would want to move from Green Bay to Los Angeles, I would want to move from Los Angeles to Florida, the guy in Florida would want to go to Minnesota. Big deal. So what? People do it every day. But their argument is, no one's going to want to play in Green Bay. They're all going to want to come out to the west coast. Well hang on a second. You go where the jobs are. And you go where they're offering the money.

'Ownership's second and probably biggest argument against free agency, was that they didn't trust each other,' said Mike Davis. 'With the profit-sharing of the television contracts, they each have an equal financial base. But with the addition of luxury box suites, some teams get richer than others. And richer teams can go after higher-priced talent. They foresee the possible back-stabbing it could cause among them.'

The union's case was strong. So strong, in fact, that management could only win by stonewalling, and manipulating the media. By turning public opinion against the union, and applying individual pressure to key players, the owners could force them into submission. But most important, unlike 1982, the owners would be prepared this time. Instead of merely

49

threatening to field teams of strikebreakers (disaffectionately known as 'scabs'), the League took definite steps to follow through. They voted unanimously to continue playing football with 'replacement players' if NFL players went out on strike. Play would be postponed for a week, and the regular season would resume on 4 October. Many teams signed players they had dropped in training camp to $1,000 retainers to be available in case of a strike.

'For the last four or five years we've been telling the membership to save, save, save,' said Davis. 'A strike could last a day, or it could last two weeks. You don't know. We arranged credit. We did our homework. As for the timing of the strike, it took two meetings to come up with a strike date. And it was not unanimous; nobody wants a strike, absolutely no one. But then we realised that we had to do it, and we (the executive committee) were the people to make that decision. We had suggestions ranging from week one, all the way to week six. But you have to understand the psychology of the player, and how that would be used against him by management. If you wait six or eight weeks, the race [to the Super Bowl] is setting up. The players now have a lot of money, of course, and can stay out longer, but – all of a sudden they're winning, they have a chance to go to the playoffs. Do the players want to screw it up? No. If Minnesota is 10 and 2, and the Chargers are 2 and 10, well I've got nothing to lose; I'm not going to the playoffs. But Minnesota is. And there are 10 to 15 teams in the playoff race. Now do those players want to sacrifice their chances for the sake of solidarity? Impossible to say for sure, but I'd guess they'd want to carry on playing. So we figured we'd strike soon enough for the negotiating sessions to be over in time to salvage the season.'

On Wednesday, 2 September, talks resumed for the first time since 14 August, amid hopes of avoiding a strike. But, after four and a half hours they broke off again, this time over the issue of protection for player representatives; a timely issue in the wake of the Brian Holloway incident.

Holloway, a three-times Pro Bowl offensive tackle for the New England Patriots, is an NFLPA vice-president and member of the union's negotiating team. On the night of Monday, 31 August (expiry date of the 1982 agreement), he

50

represented the union on national television. The following morning he was told by head coach Raymond Berry to either retire or be traded. A few hours later, he was a Los Angeles Raider, traded for a fifth-round draft choice. (When the NFL holds its annual draft of college players, each team has the right to make one selection in each of 12 rounds.) Ironically, on the day the Raiders acquired Holloway, they dropped their own player rep, Mike Davis. Perhaps management thought that three was a crowd (James Lofton is also a union rep). Said head coach Tom Flores, 'Union participation has never been an issue with us. Never.'

On Monday, 7 September, the Management Council submitted a proposal to the union that Upshaw described as 'garbage'. But the two sides agreed to meet again soon. On Tuesday, 8 September, the players voted to strike on the day after the second week of regular season games end (Tuesday, 22 September), unless there was significant progress in the negotiations. The next day, they officially rejected the 'garbage' proposal from management. The owners' response was their official decision to go on with the season, with or without the regular players.

In the meantime, the NFL continued to play the media like a master pianist. In the *New Orleans Times Picayune*, Pete Rozelle (echoed by Cleveland Browns owner Art Modell) said of the players' demand for unfettered free agency, 'I would guess if that goes off the table, they could solve the other problems rather quickly.'

On Tuesday, 15 September, the union submitted a counter-proposal to the Management Council, softening its demand for unrestricted free agency. Said Upshaw, 'All we've heard is that if players move off their demand for unfettered free agency, we can get things done. Now we'll find out if that's true.' Well, management rejected the proposal, and talks stalled once more.

Donlan and Upshaw gave the contract talks one last-ditch effort in a private meeting at Washington's National Airport, on Friday, 18 September. Donlan asked for a one-month roll-back of the union's strike date 'to give bargaining a chance'. Upshaw rejected the request, the meeting ended after two and a quarter hours, and no new bargaining session was planned before the scheduled walkout.

On Monday, 21 September, Gene Upshaw announced, 'As of midnight tonight, the players of the National Football League will be on strike again, and that's really, really sad. There's no way it can be averted. We've been forced into an action that's bad for the players, the fans and the owners. In several cities the players have already cleaned out their lockers. Others will be cleaning them out later in the week.'

According to the newspaper headlines, the issue – there was just *one* issue? – was free agency. Upshaw said, 'It's not about money, it's about dignity and freedom. It's about who you work for.'

Day One of the strike was a mixture of confusion, disappointment and determination. Ownership continued to prepare for its scab teams. Dallas Cowboys coach Tom Landry said the club's practice facility would be opened to any professional football player who wanted to show up. He also said that he could field a scab team in three or four days if he had to. The Cincinnati Bengals, Detroit Lions and Washington Redskins all reported signing between 30 and 40 free agents for their strike teams.

In Philadelphia, one of the most pro-union cities in the nation, picket signs were already prepared and hanging in the Eagles' locker room on Monday. The players set up their headquarters in a downtown AFL-CIO building.

In Washington, linebacker Neal Olkewicz, Redskins' player rep, had promised that he'd make it difficult for the scabs to get past the picket lines. But when he realised that they'd probably be brought in by bus, he said, 'That means there's nothing we can do about stopping them short of a bazooka. Maybe I'll call Rambo.'

And in Buffalo, quarterback Jim Kelly lamented, 'I wish I knew what I was going to strike about!'

Commissioner Rozelle intervened on Day One, and brought the two sides back to the bargaining table. They agreed to resume negotiations on Day Two, 23 September, in Philadelphia. Those talks went on past midnight, with a recess at 2.30 a.m., until 10 a.m. the next morning with no progress made.

Meanwhile, as 'replacement' teams organised, and picket lines began to appear around the League, the union enlisted the aid and support of local union leaders. In Los Angeles, two Raiders, player rep Sean Jones and receiver Dokie Williams, (both have since been traded), attended an AFL-CIO anniversary luncheon along with NFLPA official Doug Allen, and were assured of backing from the national union leaders. 'They're going to provide people on the picket lines to make the point to the public that the players are not alone,' said Allen. The concerns now were union-busting, scabs, job security, and freedom of choice in job opportunity.

Picket lines were up in some cities, but the atmosphere was vacation-like on many of them. No one showed up for picket duty at all in Cincinnati, Green Bay, or Minnesota. And in Miami, one lonely fan, Tim Mullin, picketed the Dolphins' training facility sitting in a folding chair under an umbrella, holding a sign that read: SCABS STAY AWAY, LET THE REAL BOYS PLAY: A FAN. But in Washington, 40 players walked picket lines at the Redskins' facility. Philadelphia and St Louis had good turnouts, and in Pittsburgh, striking players gathered at Three Rivers Stadium to make sure no one was sneaking in. In East Rutherford, New Jersey, 46 of 53 New York Giants met in the parking lot of Giants Stadium after arranging their Mercedes, Porsches and four-by-four pickup trucks in a circle like covered wagons to ensure privacy from the media.

While talks continued on Day Two, some interesting activities were reported around the League. In Buffalo, 20 striking players drove to a hotel near Rich Stadium where the scab players were being housed. Once there, a group of about five players cornered defensive back John Armstrong in the hotel's games room. One striking player had a large black dog, and Armstrong took refuge on top of a six-foot-tall video game. After talking to Armstrong for several minutes, the players left the games room, saying they were headed for the hotel's bar. Within minutes, several blue-coated security personnel and four Town of Hamburg police officers arrived at the hotel. A security officer said the players left when asked by hotel management. In Houston, the bus carrying scabs was pelted with a deadly barage of – EGGS – as it crossed the strikers' picket line. In Minnesota, Vikings officials still had not signed any 'replacement' players, so striking players said they had no reason to picket. And in Kansas City, linebacker Dino Hackett and tight end Paul Coffman waved empty shotguns and shouted: 'Where's the scabs?', while linebacker Jack

53

Del Rio and Chiefs scout Otis Taylor got into a shoving match (actually, it was more like a brawl) as Taylor attempted to escort a replacement player into the stadium. (Taylor later filed a $1 million lawsuit against Del Rio and the union.)

One particularly ironic twist on Day Two was the announcement by Ford Motor Company that it would pull its advertisements from NFL games if they were played with substitutes during the players' strike. The automobile company is owned by William Clay Ford, who is also owner of the Detroit Lions and a member of the Management Council's executive committee.

The activity continued at a moderate pace during the first ten days of the strike. There were some minor incidents on the picket lines (car windows smashed, beer bottles and eggs thrown); negotiations broke off with little or no progress (each side filed complaints against the other with the National Labour Relations Board); and the fans readied themselves for a long haul.

Scott Ostler, award-winning sports columnist for the *Los Angeles Times* predicted: 'The scab games will be enormously entertaining – to the striking players. Games will tend to look like football blooper shows. Plays will be drawn in the huddle, in the dirt. Coaches will slam a lot of headsets to the turf. Most team meetings will begin with, "This is a football. . . ." Play will be either incredibly sloppy or profoundly boring, or both. In other words, the games will be exactly like the negotiating sessions. In the end, the settlement will be a matter of supply and demand. If fans demand pro football and the owners and players don't supply it, the fans will take their business to another store. Is that the World Series I hear around the corner? College football? NBA and NHL training camps? We'll all keep busy, and you owners and players let us know when you're ready to come out and play.'

And as the replacement teams prepared for the upcoming debut of 'National ScabBall League' football games, some local writers suggested the following name changes: The Los Angeles Raiders would be the MASQUERAIDERS, the Rams would be the RAMPOSTERS. The San Francisco 49ers became the PHONY NINERS, and the San Diego Chargers would be the SAN DIEGO PICKET CHARGERS. Then we'd have the Washington REDSCABS, the Dallas CARBON

COWBOYS, the Minnesota STRIKINGS, the Kansas City CHEAPS, the Philadelphia ILLEGALS, the New England EX-PATRIOTS, the Pittsburgh STEALERS, and the Seattle CHICKEN HAWKS. Said *L.A. Times* sports columnist Mike Downey of the progress at the bargaining talks: 'A bulletin from strike negotiations has come into our newsroom – Jack Donlan just told Gene Upshaw: "Oh yeah?" And Upshaw replied: "Yeah!"'

By Day Six, the NFL media machine was pretty well cranked up. It was reported that Gene Upshaw was 'up to his rank-and-file in dissent' at the same time that he was addressing a west coast contingent of 50 players, who ended their meeting chanting 'Unity! Unity! Unity!' And each time one player crossed a picket line, it was front page (sports) news.

'We knew in the beginning that a certain percentage of players would not honour a strike, at least not for the duration,' said Mike Davis. 'We figured about 8 per cent would cross. We knew that 92 per cent would toe the line. From Day One, we were roughly 98, just a fraction below 99 per cent. Two weeks into the strike, we dropped down to about 95 per cent. The last day of the strike, we were right at 92 per cent. So we had 92 per cent of the membership on strike, standing up for what we believe in. But the way the NFL played the media, you would think that 92 per cent was in and 8 per cent was out.'

By Day Eight, results of the NFL media campaign were beginning to trickle in. A public opinion survey conducted among 1,000 American adults showed fans siding overwhelmingly with the owners rather than with the players. Some sportswriters, even, tended to lean towards the owners. But Doug Krikorian of the *Los Angeles Herald Examiner* had no such sympathies. It was the owners, he wrote, 'whose shameless greed has set in motion this whole mess, whose obvious aim is to weaken, even break the players' union, whose frugality has kept the players' salaries and pensions far below that of performers in other major sports, whose intractable stand against free agency is in arrogant defiance of long-ago court rulings that have given professional athletes the legal right to move from one team to another. Certainly, the owners will lose huge amounts of money from an extended strike, but they can endure such a financial strain because, after all, all of them are multi-millionaires with extensive holdings. The group I feel the greatest sorrow for is the players, none of whom will ever recoup the money they're losing in a strike that has all the ominous signs of deteriorating into the bitterest in sporting history.'

There were still no negotiating sessions planned. And the 'ScabBall' games were approaching. The propaganda continued: 'THE RANK AND FILE ARE BREAKING RANKS' screamed the front page of an L.A. newspaper sports section. 'Another 15 players . . . crossed picket lines yesterday. . . . That makes it 40 players on 15 teams who have returned to camps. . . .' Let's examine this briefly. Forty players on 15 teams is an average of two and a half players each, on 15 of 28 teams. Forty players from a total membership of 1,585 is 2.5 per cent. That leaves 97.5 per cent *still on strike*. Are you getting the picture?

Then came the owners' dirty tactics. In Dallas, Tony Dorsett, Cowboys star running back for the last ten years, was very vocal in his support of the union. Suddenly, he was informed by management that his annuity was in jeopardy as long as he continued to stay away from work. 'They tried the same thing with [defensive back] Everson Walls,' said Mike Davis, 'and he took their threat to the National Labour Relations Board. And he's got a case.'

But the real fireworks began on Sunday, 4 October, the first day of 'strikeball' games. Picket lines swelled to amazing proportions as thousands of union members demonstrated in support of the NFL players' strike. In Philadelphia over 30 trucks, vans, and tractor-trailer rigs blocked a street next to Veterans Stadium 45 minutes before game time. On one truck was a sign: 'Teamsters Don't Like Scabs'. There was pushing and shoving, and one car was attacked by pickets, who smashed the windshield and ripped the radio antenna off. Only 4,074 brave fans made it past the 1,500 demonstrators into the 66,592-seat stadium. In Detroit, seven people were arrested for harassing the 4,919 fans who showed up at the 80,693-seat Silverdome. In Atlanta, over 1,000 union members joined the striking players outside Atlanta-Fulton County Stadium; and in Washington, about 2,000 union members picketed Robert F. Kennedy Stadium. But the games went on. The next day, TV ratings were down, and the general consensus was that the games were disappointing, nowhere near NFL calibre, a fraud, a travesty, and basically unfortunate. Sports announcer and TV host Chris Berman said, 'It just isn't the same. These are not the top 1,600 players, they're the next 1,600. And being relatively competitive doesn't make any difference.'

Overall, fan attendance for the first weekend of 'strikeball' dropped dramatically. Stadiums that normally fill to 95 per cent of capacity were only 26 per cent filled. Seattle, Minnesota, New England and New Orleans had the lowest attendances in their clubs' history.

After the games, rumours began circulating about imminent massive defections by union members. The fact that the games were played at all seemed to discourage many players. Talks resumed, but management's claims of 'no progress' were working to intimidate and convince the players that there was no hope. Talk of expecting six to eight weeks of negotiating scared some into abandoning their stand. Additionally, owners were enticing players to return by announcing that they'd be paid for the week if they came back in by a certain time. By Day Seventeen, 8 October, 129 players had crossed picket lines. Joe Montana (quarterback, San Francisco 49ers), Dwight Clark (receiver, 49ers), Howie Long (defensive end, L.A. Raiders), Marc Wilson (quarterback, Raiders), and Ed 'Too Tall' Jones (defensive end, Dallas Cowboys) were among the more famous scabs.

Management and the union resumed negotiations on Tuesday, 6 October, and talked for six consecutive days. On Saturday, Upshaw submitted a proposal to Donlan which significantly softened the union's free agency demand. The new proposal called for teams to retain the right of first refusal by offering a free agent a 20 per cent salary increase and a one-year guaranteed contract. Compensation for lost players would be in the form of draft choices. Donlan rejected the offer, terming it a roadblock, and ended the talks on Sunday.

After the second week of 'ScabBall' had been played, the fans seemed to be warming up to the replacement players. Some of their names were becoming familiar (John Fourcade, Dwight Beverly, Vince Evans), and the stadiums were beginning to fill again.

Upshaw met with the 28 player representatives for six hours in Chicago, on Day Twenty-two of the strike, Monday, 12

October. There they agreed to end the walkout if the owners would agree in writing to submit their dispute to a federal mediator for up to six weeks; if no agreement was reached by then, the case would go to binding arbitration. But ownership said no; they would accept mediation, but not arbitration. Said one anonymous owner, 'Anytime a sports dispute has been submitted to an arbitrator, the owners have lost.' And the NFL owners weren't about to take that chance.

On Day Twenty-three, amid continuing defections, and with the threat of the only team that had remained unified in their support of the union, the Washington Redskins, reportedly ready to return *en masse*, the union announced its willingness to return to work under the 1982 agreement.

'We had players publicly putting a time frame on how long they could stay out,' said Mike Davis. 'Players saying, "Well, I'm only going to give the strike one more week." You can't *do* that! Still, there were several teams at our last meeting in Chicago that said, "Hey, we're prepared to stay out all year." There were more than 14 teams that voted to stay out all year if they had to. But then we got into the legalities of the strike and we felt that we had to do something soon. Because if we didn't, with the beating we were taking in the press. . . .

'There was a point after the first scab game was played, when we had a tremendous amount of leverage. The overnight [television] ratings were in our favour, because they were just terrible. The second week, our leverage increased – the ratings were still terrible. But you would never have known it. Because the NFL had such an effective media campaign that, even in markets where ratings were down 32 per cent, they made it seem like only 2 per cent. And the players bought that; no matter *what* we told them.

'As the weeks went on, we started receiving information about the paybacks that the owners would have to make to the TV networks under the strike provision clause in their contract, and we tried to tell the players that. Some grasped it, others didn't.

'We had several things working against us. We had lack of understanding; we had frustration; and then we had to deal with the emotional problem the players had watching someone else park in their parking slot, going into their locker stall, wearing their number, practising football, and then having the media say how great he is. That's an ugly, ugly monster to deal with.'

So on Thursday, 15 October, the National Football League Players' Association ended its strike against management. The strength and solidarity of the super-rich owners had out-muscled the lack of solidarity of the merely rich players. 'It was unfair to the players to continue to sacrifice more,' said Gene Upshaw. They returned to work *en masse*, prepared to play (and be paid for) the weekend's games. Upshaw also announced that the NFLPA had filed an antitrust lawsuit against the NFL in federal court in Minneapolis, charging, among other things, unfair industrial practices and failure to negotiate in good faith.

But the owners weren't finished yet. They had some salt to pour into the union's wound. So, when the players returned to their training facilities on Thursday, they were told that they had missed the Wednesday 10 a.m. deadline for reporting, and therefore could not play, and would not be paid for the week. 'By sundown, almost all of the strikers were back where they'd started the day – on the street.' Also, ownership would honour all the provisions of the 1982 contract, except for union dues checkoff. The union would now have to collect dues individually rather than from paycheck deductions, while it prepared for its day in court. (Sounds familiar?) And, by allowing the replacement players to play in a third NFL game, the League made them eligible to collect shares of postseason bonus money should their (?) team make the playoffs.

Well, if the players were unhappy about going out on strike, they were positively livid about the way they came back in. 'This whole damn strike doesn't make sense right now. We accomplished nothing except losing a lot of money for a lot of people,' said one irate player.

If there was a winner and a loser here, management won this one. And they did it through whatever channels they could use; obviously, their biggest weapon was the media. But I believe the NFL is going to get its comeuppance in court. They've been there many, many times before. It's been proven many times before that they are in blatant violation of the law, but they've always managed to get away somehow. How

59

do they do it? Take, for example, the case of the United States Football League (USFL). The NFL lost that case, but they only had to pay $3 in damages. Three dollars for a blatant violation of antitrust laws is a travesty of justice. It's got to catch up with them, and I think this time it will.

Chapter Six

When I saw Gary on television arguing passionately with Carl, his teammate and fellow union representative, I felt this thing must really be getting ugly. So, two friends of mine, Tommy – a musician/writer/producer and former member of an internationally famous band, and Johnny – a wide receiver/defensive back in the Arena Football League (an indoor, modified version of football), took me out to Anaheim Stadium to walk the picket lines with the guys, and get a closer look at what was going on. With the principals back at the negotiating table, I thought (hoped!) that this would be the last week of the strike, so I'd better take this opportunity to talk to the players who are most familiar to me.

I first met Gary Jeter about four or five years ago when I was a stewardess on his team's charter flights. At the time, he was dating a beautiful New York model named Leslie (whom he later married), and he rarely spoke of anything but her. He showed me a photo album with about 73,000 pictures of her in it, and with the holidays approaching, we discussed possible Christmas gifts for her (I think she got a fur coat that year). Gary struck me as a classy act; the easygoing yet dedicated type that you might not notice immediately, except that he's absolutely massive. At 6′4″ and 260 lbs, his chest and shoulders are as wide as a truck. I understand he's one of the strongest men on his team. Still, the argument caught on film by the local Channel 4 News crew seemed contrary to his personality. And I was not going to be satisfied until I'd asked him what it was about.

We got to the stadium about 10 a.m. – three hours before the scheduled contest between the Los Angeles Rams' replacement team and the Pittsburgh Steelers' replacement team. The union was very well represented. The Rams players were joined by players from the Los Angeles Raiders, former Rams currently with other teams, and some retired players. In addition, there were members from more than ten local unions walking the picket lines in support of the players.

The first person I saw was Dennis Harrah (known to his teammates as 'Herc' – short for 'Hercules'). I've always liked him but, until his marriage a couple of years ago, he was painfully candid, a notorious party person, rather intimidating (did I mention that he's an inch taller and 5 lbs heavier than Gary? – yeah), and a self-proclaimed 'redneck'. He still speaks his mind, but rumour has it he's mellowed into the family life, and prefers being at home with Theresa and baby Tanner Calvin to closing every nightclub in town. Anyway, Dennis has always been nice to me. That is, as long as he knew me only as a stewardess. Many professional athletes harbour a natural distrust of writers, and I've noticed Dennis's radar go up whenever the word 'writer' is uttered in his presence. Wanting desperately to stay on his good side (would *you* want to get on the wrong side of someone nicknamed 'Hercules'?), I decided not to try to talk to him about the strike, and – in his case at least – to speak only if and when spoken to.

Two more players, receivers Henry Ellard and Ron Brown, walked up as we were choosing signs to wear on the picket lines. Linebacker Carl Ekern, the object of Gary's televised ire, directed us to gates 7 and 9, where the stadium workers entered and the scab players' buses were expected. This is where most of the striking players were – Gary, Henry, Ron, linebacker Mike Wilcher, nose tackle Greg Meisner, and tackle Jackie Slater; guard Charley Hannah, centre Don Mosebar, and tackle Brian Holloway from the Raiders. A member of Seafarer International Union was leading chants of 'No Scabs!' and 'No Contract, No Pros!' There were men and women – just fans, with their kids – walking the line, yelling at employees who were crossing, while at the same time collecting autographs from striking players. Some of the guys were writing and shouting at the same time. They autographed picket signs, footballs and T-shirts.

After about 30 minutes, the television crews and newspaper reporters arrived and started pulling players from the line for interviews. Then came the buses carrying the scab players. There were two of them, and they stopped right in front of the entrance that the picket line was blocking. A couple of motorcycle cops appeared from nowhere and told us to make room for the buses to come through. At that point, the noise level increased dramatically. Signs were raised higher, fists started waving, and some rather unfriendly greetings were yelled. I found myself getting caught up in the emotion, and as the buses passed, I reached out and pounded on them both. Rams running back Charles White and nose tackle Alvin Wright, two of the veteran players who had crossed the line, were spotted sitting at the front of the first bus, and were called dirty bastards by their striking teammates. Charles held up two fingers in the 'peace' sign in response. At the other end of the entrance, the players got off the buses and walked towards the locker room, while the picketers continued to yell insults at them. The whole scene took about 15 minutes, then the buses backed out and were gone.

With both teams now in the stadium, Carl directed us all back to the main entrance to try and dissuade fans from going inside. More and more people were showing up, including three more striking Raiders, former Ram and current ABC sportscaster Gene Washington, and union bigwig Dave Meggyesy.

A linebacker with the St Louis Cardinals of the early '60s, Meggyesy quit the game in 1969, and wrote *Out of Their League,* a scathing indictment of the institution of football. Calling the sport 'one of the most dehumanising experiences a person can face', he was angry and disgusted with it when he left. According to David Harris, author of *The League: The Rise and Decline of the NFL,* 'Meggyesy was the first to come along and say that Pete Rozelle's attempt to portray the League as a wholesome, all-American engagement of sportsmen was incomplete. That, on one level, it was a business and a meat factory.' Now Meggyesy is the western director of the NFLPA. He seemed quite intense to me, yet, at the same time, he had a congenial, easygoing manner about him. He greeted us with firm handshakes and thanked us for our support. Then, he, Brian and Carl huddled for a conference.

It started to rain while we were picketing the main gate; lightly at first, then hard enough so that those of us who hadn't listened to the weather forecast sought refuge near the covered entrance turnstiles. One of the stadium security guys told us that we were beyond the boundaries set for picketers, and we'd have to either take off our signs or move back into the rain. We moved back into the rain. Johnny and I used our signs for cover, while Tommy went to the car to get an umbrella. Meanwhile, I spotted defensive end Reggie Doss, one of the nicest football players I know, standing under a huge double umbrella. There wasn't a *lot* of space left under there (Reggie is 6′4″, 263 lbs), but there was enough for me. So I went over to talk to him.

We chatted for a while; about the weather, about my writing. Reggie reminds me of a teddybear. He's got these round cheeks; his face looks kind of gentle. Now, just about the time I was noticing this, Ivory Sulley (a former teammate of Reggie's) walked up and said, 'Hey man! What's happenin'? I hear you guys are having a few tête-à-têtes in your team meetings.' Reggie was pleased and surprised to see him. 'Yeah man,' he answered. His expression changed, and suddenly, before my very eyes, Reggie turned into a mean old bear. 'Yeah, there were a lot of "mother-fuckers" being tossed around. And a few "sons-of-bitches" and "dirty bastards" too.' They both laughed. 'But when it was all over, we stuck together. We called each other everything in the book, but we're still a team.' Reggie's face relaxed a bit.

The rain started letting up, and then stopped. The sun suddenly appeared, and the main gate picket line began to re-form. Johnny was eavesdropping on a television interview. Tommy came back from the car. As the two of us headed back towards the line, a guy from one of the local ironworkers' unions came over to us with an open autograph book and a pen in his hand. At first I thought he was going to show us the players' signatures he'd collected. Instead, he very politely said to Tommy, 'May I have your autograph?' We glanced at each other, and neither of us was quite sure if the guy recognised Tommy as a musician, or thought he was a player. The 'what-should-I-do?' look on Tommy's face made me stare down at my feet to keep from laughing. But, being an old veteran at signing autographs for adoring fans, Tommy politely said, 'Sure!' He wrote a greeting, signed his name, and handed the book and pen back. Then the guy said, 'Oh, could you put your number down, please?' Tommy looked a little puzzled, but obligingly wrote down – his *telephone number*! The guy looked at it and smiled, looked at Tommy a little strangely, said 'Thanks a lot', and turned and walked away.

Watching all of this, I was now trying to figure out what I could do to clear up the misunderstanding without making

64

Pete Rozelle,
NFL Commissioner
(*All Sport/Mike Powell*)

A striking player
gets the message across
(*AllSport/Mike Powell*)

Above: Georgia Frontiere, owner of the LA Rams (*AllSport*)

Below: Tex Schramm, General Manager of the Dallas Cowboys (*AllSport/Trevor Jones*)

SCAB BALL IS NOT PRO BALL

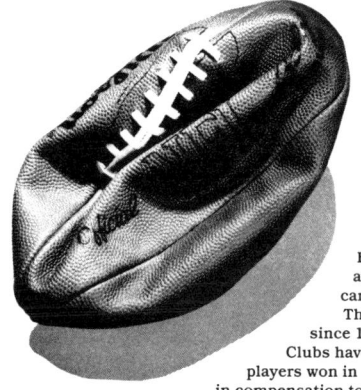

We want to watch our NFL Players Association members play football.

But they can't play without a contract. All union members understand that. And that's why we're here today.

Some of our NFLPA brothers make good money. But all 1,600 of them live with the fact that their average career length is only 3½ years and their careers could end with their next block or tackle. The owners' gross revenue has risen 100 percent since 1982. All the NFLPA is asking for is a fair agreement. Clubs have withheld $18 million in pension money that the players won in 1982. And the NFL owners are proposing cutbacks in compensation totalling $90 million in the next three years.

We don't want to be here. But we certainly will be here—every week until our NFLPA brothers are playing again. We want to watch pro ball. We'll never support scab ball.

The AFL-CIO backs the players 100 percent.

Lane Kirkland
President

Thomas R. Donahue
Secretary-Treasurer

Lynn R. Williams
President, United Steelworkers of America
Chairman, AFL-CIO Strategic Approaches Committee

| **William W. Winpisinger**
International Association
of Machinists | **John J. Sweeney**
Service Employees
International Union | **William H. Wynn**
United Food and
Commercial Workers
International Union | **Gerald W. McEntee**
American Federation
of State, County and
Municipal Employees |

A strike of national importance. This supportive circular was inserted in the newspaper *USA Today* by the American Federation of Labor, September 18, 1987

**The players
fight back:**

Todd Christiansen
of the LA Raiders
(*AllSport/Budd Symes*)

Doug Williams,
Quarter-back
for the Washington
Redskins who won
the 1988 Super Bowl
(*AllSport*)

Tommy look like a total ass. So I asked him, 'Did that guy ask for your number?' 'Yeah,' he said. 'Strange. But I gave him a fake phone number.' Well, I just couldn't hold it any longer; I broke out laughing. 'No, no, no,' I said. 'That guy thought you were a player. When he asked for your number, he meant your *jersey* number, not your telephone number!' 'Oh!' was all he could say. So we both laughed. Then I noticed that the guy hadn't gone too far away. So I walked over to him and, in my most apologetic voice, said, 'You asked my friend over there for his number, didn't you?' He said yes, and showed me Tommy's name and telephone number. I bit my lip to keep from laughing. 'Well, he's a terrible practical joker, and that phone number belongs to one of his teammates. They've been giving away each other's numbers all morning. His jersey number is 82.' The guy chuckled to himself, then wrote the number '82' below Tommy's name. He said 'Thanks. Tell Thomas I'll give him a call sometime.' 'I will!' I said, and we both laughed. I went back to Tommy and said, 'In case you decide to sign any more autographs, you're a wide receiver and your number is 82. It's a safe number. No one on the team has it. And by the way, your friend over there said to tell you he'd give you a call real soon!' We laughed as we got back into the picket line.

The first time I asked Gary about the televised argument was when we were walking the picket line near gates 7 and 9. The question had obviously been asked several times already, and he responded as if on cue: 'He said "less filling" and I said "tastes great".' (On the television commercials for Miller Lite beer, several guys are discussing the merits of the product. Half of them say it's less filling, the other half say it tastes great. The discussion turns into a near riot.) I looked up at him in a way that said, 'Stop pulling my leg and tell me what happened,' and he looked down at me in a way that said, 'That's all I'm saying.' So we kept on walking.

Chapter Seven

During the strike of 1987, if there was one thing that all sides agreed on, it was the plight of the coaches. Caught in the middle of the power struggle between the players and the owners, the coaches were expected to field teams of replacement players after just one week of practice together. Some coaches did an admirable job, considering what they were given to work with. Others, caught completely unprepared, suffered through three frustrating weeks of watching their replacement players struggle aimlessly on the field, while their regular players walked picket lines. Still others, who had looked ahead and prepared for the probable, enjoyed victories they'd never known before.

Take, for example, the story of the New Orleans Saints. Here is a team that has never, in its entire 21-year history, *never* had a winning season. In 1987 they earned their first-ever playoff berth, with a record of 12 wins and three losses. Three of those victories were had by the strike-breaking replacement team. Owner Tom Benson began prancing up and down the sidelines after each victory, and soon, the 'Benson Boogie' was the rage of New Orleans.

Then there was the New York Giants. The defending Super Bowl Champions, looking to repeat their championship season, wound up watching the playoffs on television with the rest of us. Their replacement team lost all three of its games, and then, along with the regular players' two pre-strike losses, handed them a record of no wins and five losses.

You had to feel badly for the coaches. For six, sometimes seven consecutive months, they work extraordinarily long days, drawing up game plans and practice schedules; always looking for the edge that will win the next game. Sometimes they sleep over in their offices, analysing films for countless hours. Often, a coach's children seem to grow up behind his back.

So much of a coach's life is his football team that, when the threat of a players' strike became a reality, many of them were (understandably) upset. Jim Mora, head coach of the New Orleans Saints said, 'I'm disappointed because we've spent all this time getting our guys prepared for the season, and now we can't have them.' Mike Ditka, the Chicago Bears' head coach, was quite animated: 'It takes all the fun out of it. You feel frustrated. Everybody talks about how they've been betrayed. I feel like the coaching staff, the organisation, has been betrayed. I feel like the memory of George Halas (the Bears' founder) has been betrayed; 63 years of history have been betrayed.' Green Bay Packers head coach Forrest Gregg didn't even want to talk about it at first: 'I have no feelings. I have to finish working on some films.' But then they all re-signed themselves, grudgingly, to the situation. Los Angeles Raiders head coach Tom Flores stated with a noted lack of enthusiasm, 'According to a directive from the Management Council, we're obliged to field a team. If we didn't do this, we would be subject to a substantial fine or the loss of draft choices.' And poor Mike Ditka. One would have thought for a moment that he was going to have a nervous breakdown. 'I'm not strong enough mentally to do what they're asking us to do,' he said. 'But I'm going to try.'

In Dallas, Cowboys head coach Tom Landry was certain that he could field a replacement team in three or four days if necessary. 'Remember, we were scrimmaging the Los Angeles Raiders after three days in training camp,' he said. Rookie head coach Frank Gansz of the Kansas City Chiefs was a little uncertain: 'We're going to make the very best of the situation. I think teams in heavily populated areas will have the advantage, because they have a lot of players – Los Angeles, Philadelphia, New York. Lots of very good football players live in the San Diego–Los Angeles area. Nobody said it was always going to be fair.' Both Bill Parcells in New York and Dan Reeves in Denver seemed frustrated – maybe because they felt a bit helpless. 'I don't have any control over the situation, including the procurement of players. I am just playing with the cards I was dealt,' said Parcells. Coach Reeves agreed, 'It's difficult to prepare when you don't know what to prepare for.' John Robinson, head coach of the Los Angeles Rams explained further, 'I find myself in a weird position. We are obviously committed to our football team. We represent management, but we also want to have a strong and positive relationship with our players. There is no contract and the players clearly have a right to strike. I think one of the major problems in all this is everybody wants to perceive what's right and wrong. I don't think there is that. There clearly are rights. If a player chooses not to work, that's his choice. If an owner wants to field another team, that's his (or her) right.

'I'm thinking Gene Upshaw and Jack Donlan might go into the men's room underneath the stands and settle this at half-time – now there's a solution!

'I just think it's very difficult to know what to do. What would I do if my coaches were going to strike? We've had a pretty close team here. A lot of them are pretty good friends. I'd hate to see those things destroyed.'

Coach Ray Perkins of the Tampa Bay Buccaneers held out hope that the regulars would return soon: 'I think at the end of this week, or certainly after this first replacement game, some of the striking players will start trickling in. All of them are affected differently because they get paid differently. Some are hurt worse than others.'

But Pittsburgh's Chuck Noll, a veteran coach with over 30 years of NFL experience, has been through this before. 'There's always optimism at the beginning, the players aren't going to miss much time, the strike's not going to be long. But it seems that once the union gets them out on strike, they keep them on strike.'

So in 1987 National Football League coaches did as they were told, and after four weeks of training camp, four weeks of exhibition games and two regular season games, they went back to the drawing board and began all over again. Jim Mora tried to stay positive: 'As always, we're looking to put together the very best possible players we can. We can do it. Our system may be limited, but the people we will be playing are in the same boat we're in. Everybody is starting from zero, so we'll see what happens. We'll probably go out in shorts and helmet and find out who's who. It'll be just like guys starting out. We won't be preparing for an opponent tomorrow.'

Tom Flores, however, was having a rather difficult time warming up to the idea. 'I can't comment on the calibre of the people we have here. This is not something of my doing, this whole situation. We've been mandated to field a team, and since the league stated that these games are going to count, you can bet your life we're going to be as competitive as possible. We're 2–0 right now, and we certainly don't want to slip. So we're going to give it our best shot. Obviously it's not going to be totally refined football because it's impossible to do that in just ten days. But we will be as competitive as we possibly can. We've reached back for as many players as possible who were in training camp so that the learning time is minimized. We'll find out if these guys are of NFL calibre. A lot of them have made some impression. That's why we invited them to camp in the first place. We have taken players before who hadn't had a home, and they've turned out OK for us. I think they all have a dream, and this is probably their opportunity to fulful that dream of playing with a National Football League team even if it is for only a short time.'

Raiders assistant coach Sam Gruneisen added: 'We're keeping it pretty simple. We've asked them to learn each others' names and where they're supposed to stand on the field. We don't want to go too fast, or we'll lose some of them mentally. Of course, we've already lost them physically, or they wouldn't be available.' In Miami, assistant coach David Shula said, 'We've gone from trying to prepare for Lawrence Taylor [superstar linebacker with the New York Giants] to showing people how to line up in the huddle.' His dad, head coach Don Shula continued, 'We've got some players who just missed making our team. These should be high-calibre players. But we have others who are not in the best shape and others who are not good enough to play in the NFL. Certainly we're going to have to gear down. We won't be as sophisticated as we normally are.'

And in Los Angeles, coach Robinson simply hoped for the best: 'We have a small squad, so we don't want to wear them down real fast. We'd like them to do everything as quickly as possible – keep fresh, learn as much as they can, and know the team prayer. Those are probably the three things that are the most important part of this whole thing. You look at this different ways. You'd hate to go down and play somebody who has 15 of their players with none of your own. We're 0 and 2 and we can't afford to slip further off the pace. That's my concern.'

Once they started practising, coaches around the League got a better look at what they had. Cowboys assistant coach

Paul Hackett actually enjoyed it: 'You can't help but get caught up in the novelty of this. These games won't be in the ballpark of the NFL, but they don't have to be. The kids are so enthusiastic – it's their chance at a dream. They're fun to coach.' Meanwhile, more than ever before, there was definitely parity in the NFL. 'We don't know what the opponent will be like, and they don't know what we'll be like. There'll be some mistakes made. There always are early in the season, and this is as early as you can get.' Defensive co-ordinators John Paul Young of the Kansas City Chiefs and Bill Belichick of the New York Giants agreed that the complicated NFL defences presented a special challenge to their replacement players. 'It's pretty obvious the situation we're in when you bring in guys and ask them to play defences they don't even know the names of,' said Young. 'It's a lot different. We won't even have time for some of the basic defences and techniques we usually prepare,' added Belichick.

Then came 'Strikeball' – week one, two and three. No one knew quite what to expect, and curiosity was consistently high. Fans throughout the country responded differently – as many showed up in Denver and Dallas as stayed away in Philadelphia and St Louis. Some were surprised by genuinely entertaining football; others were bored to tears by talentless ineptitude.

Coach Robinson tried to remain calm: 'We clearly fell short with this group and we'd have to make marked improvement to be competitive in the long term. Had we gone back and signed the top 20 or 25 from our training camp and assembled that, we might have been OK. But we were slow and did not manage it, which was a setback for us.' Fritz Shurmur, Robinson's defensive co-ordinator added, 'They're not the same calibre games. The 1,500 players in this League are the best accumulated over a 13–14-year period, with all the time and coaching put into them. If these games continue, it will take more than a fist to close the hole in the dyke.' 'I don't think the League can stand this much longer,' said Robinson. 'I had the impression that the fans had fun at the game, but would they come back next week if their team lost?'

After his first 'strikeball' loss, Philadelphia head coach Buddy Ryan was not quite so kind: 'I'd trade this whole group with *anybody* – sight unseen!' This strike, he said, was the 'roughest time I've ever had in 31 years of coaching'. Then he added, 'I think the fans were entertained, but it was not very entertaining for me. I just want to get the (regular) Eagles back in there.' Tom Flores concurred. His 'Masqueraiders' lost two of the three games while he searched in vain for some rhythm, some consistency, maybe even a little logic. 'We are a sport that lives by film,' he said. 'We study film constantly. We all but take film to bed with us. Looking at film, we learn the system of the opponent and we learn the habits of the players. But what's to learn today? The lineups keep changing and you don't have the slightest idea what the opposing coach, in desperation, is going to come up with next.'

Jim Mora, on the other hand, was having heretofore unknown success in New Orleans. He said of his replacement players, 'Their progress is amazing. They looked like a football team out there today. They have a way to go, but these games might surprise you. You're probably going to see better football than you think.'

Still, three weeks was more than enough for all the coaches. When the strike ended on 15 October, a collective sigh of coaches' relief could be heard around the League. Said Mike Ditka, 'It's the greatest feeling in the world that they're coming back.'

The owners' decision not to allow the returning players to participate in that week's games was not a very popular one among the coaches. With Buddy Ryan, it was difficult to determine which he was happier about: the regular players returning or the replacement players leaving. 'We could have the striking players ready to play this week. It would be easier than getting the replacements ready.' And in New England, head coach Raymond Berry was a reluctant messenger: 'I asked them, "Didn't you know that one o'clock yesterday was the deadline? Did any of you understand that?" Nobody said anything, then I affirmed they couldn't play this week.' Both Forrest Gregg in Green Bay and Jim Mora in New Orleans, whose replacement teams won two of the three games, bade those teams a fond farewell. 'The one thing I can say about these players is that they gave a full and honest effort at all time,' said Gregg. 'I'm proud of the job these players have done in three games for us,' added Mora. 'I'm happy to see the strike is over, but these replacement players did a heck of a job.'

While everyone was aware of the sensitive issues surrounding the players' return, most were confident of eventually working them out. Coach Robinson's team was noticeably splintered after the strike, and he addressed that issue immediately and publicly. 'I don't think there's any room for disunity in any club that pretends to want to compete. Disunity is fatal. If a club chooses that, they are no longer a team.' In a different vein, Joe Gibbs' Washington Redskins, the only team to remain 100 per cent together throughout the strike, had a private team meeting with their coach. 'The meeting was between me and them,' said Gibbs, 'and we're gonna be working our way through a tough situation to get over this whole episode. I was glad to see the guys and get a chance to talk to them.'

So most of the NFL's coaches survived the strike of '87. Some had a few extra grey hairs, and there were a couple of casualties: Forest Gregg left Green Bay for a colleage coaching job, and Tom Flores resigned in Los Angeles. Still, the National Football League goes on. Next year, the coaches will start all over again teaching, planning, strategising. There will be mini-camps and training camps and preseason exhibition games. We'll say hello to some new stars, and so-long to some old friends. And let's hope, for the sake of the fans as well as the coaches, that we won't ever have to suffer through another replacement season again.

Chapter Eight

Many players, both active and retired, had strong opinions on the strike of 1987. Others were either uninformed, indifferent, or both, and had little, if anything to say about it. From Day One of the strike until well after it was over, I gathered a variety of answers to a variety of questions from a variety of players:

WHAT ARE YOUR FEELINGS ON THE ISSUE AT STAKE?
Mark Malone, quarterback, Pittsburgh Steelers I don't think free agency is worth striking for.
Jim Kelly, quarterback, Buffalo Bills We don't know what's going on. I wish I knew what I was going to strike about.
Charles Mann, defensive end, Washington Redskins We are going out over pensions and severance, not free agency.
Danny White, quarterback, Dallas Cowboys I'm in agreement with most of the issues the union is after, but I'm not in agreement with the methods being used.
Ron Wooten, offensive guard, New England Patriots If Upshaw can't get them resolved in a hurry, we want someone else who can.

DO YOU AGREE WITH THE STRIKE?
Nate Newton, offensive lineman, Dallas Cowboys I think all of it stinks, but I gotta go with it.
Hoby Brenner, tight end, New Orleans Saints I really thought we'd get this thing settled without walking; I was hoping both sides had learned their lessons in 1982.
Keith Fahnhorst, offensive tackle, San Francisco 49ers Apparently both sides are stupid enough to get into this situation.
Sean Jones, defensive end, Los Angeles Raiders This is so ridiculous, especially for this team. Our owner doesn't want to strike. Neither do the players. But you've got to do what you've got to do.

73

Stan Brock, offensive tackle, New Orleans Saints As far as we're concerned they've forced us to strike. There's nobody in the NFL who's saying, "Hey, that's great! We'll get some time off!" We don't want to strike. But we support our union. We're solid.

Tony Elliott, defensive lineman, New Orleans Saints I believe we could get better pensions, better contracts, better benefits without striking.

Rusty Hilger, quarterback, Los Angeles Raiders Right now I think it's in my best interest that I don't say a word.

HOW DO YOU THINK THE FANS FEEL ABOUT THE STRIKE?

Bernie Kosar, quarterback, Cleveland Browns Gene has told us that fan sentiment isn't as big a deal as some people say it is, but I feel the fans do play a big role in the whole nature of professional football. A group of us were at a hockey game the other night, and the fans really let us have it. We got booed a lot and it bothered us. To say that these people aren't involved in the strike is wrong.

Mike Davis, defensive back, LA Raiders/San Diego Chargers We didn't come out here just to stand still. We want to move. It's obvious fan participation wasn't there. The owners are astute businessmen. They know it took 67 years for fan support to build. They don't want to see it go away in two weeks.

Jeff Rohrer, linebacker, Dallas Cowboys It's unbelievable how the management in Dallas has cowed the fans. I can't believe the people in Dallas would be so stupid that they would be led by the nose for these last three weeks. Guys are so sick that they are talking about moving out of Dallas during the off-season.

WHAT DO YOU THINK ABOUT THE REPLACEMENT GAMES?

Mike Lansford, kicker, Los Angeles Rams The scabs – what they've done is unify us. Management has done more for unity with that insult than they possibly could have known.

Doug Cosbie, tight end, Dallas Cowboys This is not pro football. I'd rather see the fans give $25 to charity and get a tax writeoff.

74

Neal Olkewicz, linebacker, Washington Redskins I never thought they'd get these games going. I thought it was just intimidation.

James Jones, running back, Detroit Lions This could really turn the fans off. They're turned off as it is.

Sean Jones, defensive end, Los Angeles Raiders When you're desperate, you resort to desperate measures, and playing games with scabs would be a desperate measure.

Brian Bosworth, linebacker, Seattle Seahawks The fans aren't going to go for that. They're paying big money to see superstars play, not sandlot football. The owners are just insulting the fans' intelligence.

Brian Holloway, offensive tackle, NE Patriots/LA Raiders The American public doesn't come to see the powers or the people dressed up in team jerseys. It's the NFL talent and abilities and personalities that they're interested in.

HOW DO YOU FEEL ABOUT THE SCAB PLAYERS?

Steve DeOssie, linebacker, Dallas Cowboys It doesn't bother me they'll get playoff shares. The owners have to pay the money anyway. It doesn't come out of our pockets. Sure, I hope the replacements whip the Redskins but I won't be at the game cheering.

Steve Jordon, tight end, Minnesota Vikings Guys coming in here as scabs would have to deal with their own consciences. Obviously, we're not going to take them to our bosom.

Henry Ellard, receiver, Los Angeles Rams I wouldn't hold any hard feeling against someone who crossed a picket line. As for other players, I can't speak for them.

Mel Owens, linebacker, Los Angeles Rams I'm from Detroit. I grew up with UAW (United Auto Workers) and Teamsters. It gets to be a pretty ugly business. When the Teamsters went on strike, people were being shot on the highway. It's hard to be out here and see people take your job.

Boomer Esiason, quarterback, Cincinnati Bengals I'd sure hate to be one of those scabs in our camp next summer.

Todd Christensen, tight end, Los Angeles Raiders When I was standing out there picketing, I looked down at my feet. I realised I'd had three broken bones in my feet, and I started to think about the rest of my body. I thought to myself that it's taken ten years to get to this point. Now because of an industrial dispute, someone can not only take my place, but when this thing is over, some of these people are going to be on the roster and they're going to get the benefits I've risked my career to get. How ironic, how incredible, and how unjust.

Albert Lewis, defensive back, Kansas City Chiefs I try not to judge, just as I don't want to be judged. He has as much right to be in there as I do to picket. The guys who are picketing are picketing as a team, and the guys who choose to cross it are doing it as a team. They have one objective, and we have another.

Dave Rimington, centre, Cincinnati Bengals If they're a part of the team, I guarantee you'll have a wedge driven through this team. Any chance of our being successful will be diminished.

HOW DO YOU FEEL ABOUT THE VETERANS WHO CROSSED THE PICKET LINES?

Mike Quick, receiver, Philadelphia Eagles We'll just let them know we're here and that they're interfering with our livelihood; that we're trying to make it better for all of them.

Dave Puzzuoli, defensive tackle, Cleveland Browns With friends like these, who needs enemies?

Brad Edelman, offensive guard, New Orleans Saints It's not a good situation when those guys cross, but it's still only a small percentage of the club.

Deron Cherry, defensive back, Kansas City Chiefs I can't see how I could play along with someone like that. They're cutting our throats. How can I depend on someone like that during the season? I want someone who's going to be in the battle with me and who's going to fight, and that's what a team is made of.

Mark Malone, quarterback, Pittsburgh Steelers If you can't be loyal to yourself and your teammates, who can you be loyal to? I find it very, very difficult to sell my buddies out. My position is such that you have to depend on ten other guys you play with to all perform their jobs well so you have a chance to get your job done. We can't have factions, can't have people splitting in all different directions and having animosity towards each other. The only way you can win on the field is to have a real tight-knit bunch of guys. You have anything but that, you're going to have real problems.

WHY DID YOU CROSS THE PICKET LINE?

Jerry Robinson, linebacker, Los Angeles Raiders I held out as long as I could. I showed my loyalty to the players' union. Now it's time to come back in.

Mervyn Fernandez, Receiver, Los Angeles Raiders It was just time to come back.

Greg Townsend, defensive end, Los Angeles Raiders I called guys some names last week, and here I am. I started thinking about coming back right after the deadline last week. I'd heard the strike was just about over, and then it seemed to be back at square one. That was it, as far as I was concerned.

James Campen, centre, New Orleans Saints Financially, I couldn't swing it. I took time to make this decision. I showed my feeling for the union by staying out a week. But at the same time, I've got to show some loyalty to my employer. They gave me a chance last year when nobody drafted me. Loyalty to my boss means something too.

Doug Flutie, quarterback, New England Patriots I don't know whether what I'm doing is right or wrong. I just know the best thing for Doug Flutie is to come here and play.

John Gesek, offensive lineman, Los Angeles Raiders I'm a tenth-round draft choice. I didn't get a $300,000 bonus. I'm getting married in June. I stayed out as long as I could. I can't afford to stay out any longer.

Dwight Clark, receiver, San Francisco 49ers I didn't realise everyone felt that strongly. We'll see how they feel next week after they miss another paycheck.

Mike Lansford, kicker, Los Angeles Rams I thought I might as well play and help the team because I think the union is going to collapse this week.

ED GARVEY SAID IN 1982 THAT, CONSIDERING THE REASONS GIVEN BY PLAYERS WHO CROSSED THE PICKET LINES, THE NFL MUST BE AN ASSOCIATION OF BACHELORS; NO ONE ELSE HAD A FAMILY, RIGHT?

Howie Long, defensive lineman, Los Angeles Raiders We did what we felt was right for our families and the future of our families. Basically, that's it.

Gary Hogeboom, quarterback, Indianapolis Colts I've

got some things in my contract that are too important to my family and myself. That's the bottom line.

Steve Korte, centre, New Orleans Saints In one way, I wish I could support the players, because I am a player too. But I have to do what's right for my family. I have to stand on my own two feet.

Steve Largent, receiver, Seattle Seahawks At this time I feel my commitment to maintain team unity potentially threatens my ability to provide for my family's wellbeing, although there are many, many other mitigating factors.

Alvin Wright, nose tackle, Los Angeles Rams I got a family and this is my job. If that's a problem, they'll have to deal with it.

HOW DO YOU FEEL ABOUT THE UNION? HOW SOLID IS IT?

Charley Hannah, offensive lineman, Los Angeles Raiders The reports of our death are greatly exaggerated.

Henry Ellard, receiver, Los Angeles Rams What we've been through with the Rams is what the union is trying to prevent – us getting nothing.

HOW UNIFIED HAS YOUR TEAM REMAINED DURING THE STRIKE?

Sean Jones, defensive lineman, Los Angeles Raiders I believe we've stayed together. We've had a lot of guys go in, yes, but there are more guys out than in, and that's what is important. As long as you have more bullets on your side than they have on their side, then you stand a chance of outshooting them.

Ricky Hunley, linebacker, Denver Broncos We play as a team, we win as a team, we lose as a team, we will go out as a team.

John Elway, quarterback, Denver Broncos My main concern is to keep everyone together on the team. I worked four years to gain the respect of this team, and I want to keep it. We voted as a team to strike and not to cross a picket line. Whether I believe in it or not, I'm going to go the way we voted as a team.

HOW HAS THE STRIKE AFFECTED YOU?
Dennis Harrah, offensive guard, Los Angeles Rams I lost $100,000. I got a black eye. But I got just a little bit of dignity left. I'm holding on to that little bit of dignity and hoping that my creditors will take dignity as credit, 'cause I damn sure don't have that hundred grand.

WHAT ARE YOUR THOUGHTS ON THE END OF THE STRIKE?
Dennis Harrah offensive guard, Los Angeles Rams The strike is over; let's not fool ourselves. This is a chance for a few guys to make money.

Ricky Hunley, linebacker, Denver Broncos The thing was falling apart. It was like being in a war and losing your bullets. There was nothing left to fight with. The bottom was falling out of the situation. I don't think anybody won. I'll just be happy to get back on the playing field.

Chris Collinsworth, receiver, Cincinnati Bengals It's the end of the Civil War, and the owners are taking Atlanta. We're trying to get the furniture out before it burns.

Bob Golic, nose tackle, Cleveland Browns We made a sacrifice for something we believe in. It's not exactly the way we anticipated it ending, so obviously I'm disappointed. We're egomaniacs. Professional athletes are egotistical, and they have to be that way. Right now, a lot of these guys want to find a way to get their self-respect back. They don't like getting kicked in the tail.

James Lofton, receiver, Los Angeles Raiders The thing is, when you start a game, you play it as hard as you can. That's what we attempted to do. We may have fallen a little bit short. It'll be tough at first but it's like anything else. You work together, you work in very close quarters and you have to get the job done. There are friendships that took a slap in the face, but a lot of times those can be mended.

Linden King, linebacker, Los Angeles Raiders We're beat. We got beat and that's all there is to it.

Steve DeOssie linebacker, Dallas Cowboys It doesn't make sense, but this whole damn strike doesn't make sense right now. We accomplished nothing except losing a lot of money for a lot of people.

Billy Ray Smith, linebacker, San Diego Chargers You get a little tired of kicking the neighbourhood dogs and throwing tomatoes at the kids. It's nice to be back.

Bill Haas, defensive lineman, Kansas City Chiefs We're back in as a team and we have absolutely nothing. We've run up the white flag. There's a good chance we can lose everything and the union can go under. We wanted to get ready for Sunday's game. They told us we couldn't even use the field to practise on until the scabs were finished. I went down to the locker room, just to get my mail, and the scabs scurried around like rats. It was the sorriest sight I'd ever seen. There's so much power, litigation and ego involved in this thing, you can't begin to imagine what this strike is all about. This isn't what I pictured a career as a pro football player would be like when I was in the eighth grade.

THE STRIKE HAS ENDED, BUT THE OWNERS WILL NOT LET THE REGULARS PLAY. YOUR THOUGHTS ON THAT?

Neal Olkewicz, linebacker, Washington Redskins We have been told that we cannot play. We will not get paid. Therefore, we are on strike again. It's as simple as that.

Ali Haji-Sheikh, kicker, Washington Redskins What happened today is just a microcosm of what the whole strike has been about. The owners tell us whatever the hell they want to tell us, and we've got to abide by it.

Dan Marino, quarterback, Miami Dolphins We're ready to work. They don't want us to work.

William Judson, defensive back, Miami Dolphins The players would rather play the game. We're trying to give the fans what they want to see – the real football players – but we're being rejected. The owners are playing hardball with us.

Hoby Brenner, tight end, New Orleans Saints We work for our salaries; it's as simple as that. We tried to go in without an agreement. They don't want us back.

Ron Heller, offensive tackle, Tampa Bay Buccaneers Management is treating us like puppy dogs coming back with our tails between our legs and tossing us a bone and patting us on the head.

HOW DO YOU FEEL ABOUT YOUR JOB, AND ABOUT NFL MANAGEMENT NOW?

Harry Carson, linebacker, New York Giants I think they have played hardball since the whole process began. It's everyone's opinion that they were out all along to bust the union, humble the players somewhat. It's a little like when you have a person down, and you grind your foot into them. I think that's what they are trying to do.

Dan Hampton, defensive end, Chicago Bears The world is not fair. If the world was fair, kids would not get cancer and owners would not treat players like pieces of meat. It's not a sport any more. It's a business.

WHY DO YOU THINK THE UNION LOST THE STRIKE?

Jim McMahon, quarterback, Chicago Bears Hey, we were the bad guys because we had nil PR from our union. That's where the owners had us by the short hairs. The fans shouldn't have been against us, but they were, because the owners poured on the PR. It was a smart move on their part.

HOW DO YOU FEEL THIS STRIKE HAS AFFECTED THE INSTITUTION OF AMERICAN PROFESSIONAL FOOTBALL?

Mick Luckhurst, kicker, Atlanta Falcons I think a tremendous amount. And that's why the players made the move they did. A vast majority of players and player reps did not want to go back to work. But they saw that the game was being hurt, the fan was being hurt, individual owners were being hurt, and it just kept going round and round and round and we said, let's just end this. I think the League has been hurt.

David Hill, tight end, Los Angeles Rams The repercussions of this strike are worse than in 1982. Then, we just lost money. The division of teams, it will take us a long time to overcome.

Gary Danielson, quarterback, Cleveland Browns The timing was bad and the strategy was bad. The atmosphere in the United States right now is pro-business and anti-union. As a result, we lost. We also lost friendships, team unity and fans. We also lost for other pro athletes in baseball, basketball, hockey. I don't know how long it will take to get it all together again.

Chapter Nine

I had a dream two nights after the strike was officially over. In it, several men and one woman were gathered around a large conference table. The strike had ended, and the participants and some objective observers were discussing what had happened, where the NFL stands now, and where it could be heading. I could not make out what they were saying in my dream, so when I woke up I designed a scenario which, while fictional, is still quite true to life.

The setting is a conference room on the 17th floor of the Crystal City Marriott Hotel, near Washington's National Airport. It is four days since the union ordered the striking football players back to work. Commissioner Pete Rozelle has called for this meeting of all concerned parties, in an attempt to hammer out some sort of viable working arrangement that everyone can live with. He has very high hopes.

The room is elegant and simple. The walls are mahogany-panelled. A five-foot-wide crystal chandelier hangs majestically above a 20-foot oval mahogany conference table. Around the table are 15 high-backed chairs with deep wine-coloured kid leather seats. On the table, in front of the ten chairs closest to the door – five on each side – are Waterford crystal water goblets (Powers Court pattern), sterling silver ashtrays, and leather-bound notebooks containing the meeting's agenda. Those chairs are occupied by the Movers and Shakers of the National Football League.

Sitting at the end of the table closest to the entrance (and exit), and presiding over the meeting, is NFL Commissioner Alvin 'Pete' Rozelle. Making his first public appearance since the college draft, Pete looks, at first glance, tanned and fit. The light from the chandelier dances through the hanging crystal and catches Pete's thinning silver-tinged hair. Upon closer inspection, however, one might notice the worn, haggard look in Pete's eyes; the result of over 15 years of fighting, turmoil, and court battles involving the NFL.

Pete Rozelle, a polished public relations wizard, assumed the position of Commissioner of the National Football League on the evening of 26 January 1960. His name had been submitted as a 'compromise candidate' after the 12 owners had spent ten days disagreeing on a suitable replacement for the recently deceased commissioner, Bert Bell. On a motion by Carroll Rosenbloom (then owner of the Baltimore Colts), seconded by Paul Brown (then general manager and head coach of the Cleveland Browns), at 10.35 p.m. the National Football League voted eight for Rozelle, with three abstentions and one against.

The media called him 'the boy Czar', and 'League Think' became the lynchpin, the 'central ideology' of his administration. The premise of 'League Think' is solidarity; unity of purpose; one for all and all for one. The central issue in the '60s was television. Rozelle proposed that the NFL should sell its collective TV rights as a single package and share its broadcasting revenue equally among all franchises. Then, realising that such an arrangement might constitute an illegal monopoly, he spent the summer of 1961 lobbying the United States Congress for an exemption from the Sherman Antitrust Act. What he got, in the September of that year, was a Sports Antitrust Broadcast Act, which allows sports leagues to pool and sell their TV rights.

Pete has spent a great deal of the past 15 years lobbying Congress for a blanket exemption from the antitrust laws. In the meantime, he has faced several lawsuits and three strikes, all citing the NFL's blatant violations. 'Litigation has become a way of life for me,' he has said. 'It's an unpleasant way of life, but I'm inured to it now. We get sued all the time.' Now, however, sorting through the ashes of the 1987 players' strike, Pete is desperately seeking a way of avoiding another merry-go-round in the courts. He is tired, and he knows that with just one 'wrong' ruling, 'Our league and everything it does could be found illegal.'

Seated to the left of the commissioner is Tex Schramm, president of the Dallas Cowboys, and one of football's acknowledged experts. Schramm sits on the Executive Committee of the League's Management Council (which handles negotiations with the union on behalf of all 28 franchises), and wields considerable power and influence inside the NFL.

Tex and Pete go a long way back. They met in the early '50s when Schramm was general manager of the Los Angeles Rams, and Rozelle was athletic news director at the University of San Francisco. Schramm hired Rozelle as the Rams' public relations director in 1952, and Pete took over as general manager when Tex resigned in 1957.

Often referred to as 'Mr Vice-Commissioner', Schramm was outspoken and firm in the League's resolve before, during and after this most recent strike. He projected the hard-line stance that the League took during negotiations, never wavering, and engineering a decisive victory.

Seated to the right of the commissioner is Hugh Culverhouse, a Florida tax attorney, and owner of the Tampa Bay Buccaneers. Hugh is chairman of the NFL Management Council's executive committee, and has also attained a great deal of power within the NFL, considering the relatively short period of time (13 years) that he has been a member of the League.

His entrance into the NFL had a rather 'back-door' style to it. In June of 1972, he bid for, and thought he had successfully purchased, the Los Angeles Rams from the estate of recently deceased owner Dan Reeves. Instead, he found that Carroll Rosenbloom (who had become 'bored with Baltimore') had worked a last-minute deal in which Chicago heating contractor Robert Irsay would buy the Rams for $2 million more than Culverhouse had offered, and then trade the entire franchise to Rosenbloom for the Colts and $4 million cash. Pete Rozelle and the NFL approved the deal, so Culverhouse took them all to court, charging violations of the Sherman Antitrust Act in their attempt 'to further monopolize the monopoly power acquired by them in the business of professional football'. It was, according to Culverhouse, 'monopoly power attained illegally'.

Well, the case was settled before it reached trial. In a 'meeting of minds' between Rosenbloom and Culverhouse, Hugh agreed to drop his lawsuit, and Carroll agreed to work 'behind the scenes' on Hugh's behalf when expansion came along.

When the League expanded into Tampa and Seattle in 1974, the Tampa franchise was awarded to Thomas McCloskey, a Philadephia contractor. The Seattle franchise was offered to Culverhouse, but after his experience with the Rams, he decided he didn't want to live on the west coast after all, and turned the offer down. One month later, McCloskey backed out of the Tampa deal, and Culverhouse was selected to replace him.

By 1977, Hugh was sitting on two very important NFL committees – the Congressional Relations Committee and the Finance Committee – and his tax-consulting services had been hired by several League members. After Carroll Rosenbloom's death in 1978, Culverhouse became executor of the Rosenbloom estate.

On Hugh's right is Georgia Frontiere, widow of Carroll Rosenbloom, and owner of the Los Angeles Rams. Georgia got her franchise the old-fashioned way – she inherited it.

Sometimes referred to as 'Madam Ram', Georgia's initiation into the fraternity that is the National Football League was a rocky one which left her defensive, camera-shy, and ever-leery of the press.

She was an aspiring opera singer who often entertained her husband and their guests with songs after dinner. She was also a dutiful wife who was kept completely out of the operation of her husband's football team. Rosenbloom forbade Georgia to come to the Rams' offices, and even to sit in the owner's box during home games. All of that changed when the Rams became hers.

Georgia entered the NFL as the first woman to control 100 per cent of a professional football team. She also entered with what appeared to be reckless abandon; making unpopular decisions which made her football knowledge a League-wide joke. After much trial and many errors, she quietly slipped into the background of the football operations, and refused to talk to reporters.

One person she *does* talk to, however, is Hugh Culverhouse. As executor of her late husband's estate, as well as a trusted financial advisor, Hugh has a close relationship with Georgia. In 1980 one Los Angeles newspaper stated that, 'It's now quite apparent that Hugh Culverhouse is playing a prominent role with the Rams, and that Georgia Frontiere doesn't make a major move without consulting him.'

Across the table from Georgia and to the left of Tex Schramm is Jack Kent Cooke, owner of the Washington Redskins. Probably the richest man in the league, his media empire –

including newspapers, radio stations and cable TV – is valued at over $900 million.

A multi-talented sports entrepreneur, Cooke bought into professional football in 1961. For $350,000, he bought 25 per cent of the Redskins' holding company, Pro Football, Inc. Four years later he bought the National Basketball Association's Los Angeles Lakers. The next year he bought the Los Angeles Kings, a National Hockey League expansion franchise. Then he spent $16 million building the Fabulous Forum in Inglewood, California. The arena, dismissed as 'Cooke's folly' when it was first announced, housed his Lakers and his Kings, and made money from the day it opened.

But since NFL policy prohibits cross-ownership in any other sports, Cooke finally agreed in May 1979 to sell his basketball and hockey teams, as well as his Forum. Since then, he has lived like a country squire on his 50-acre estate (Fallingbrook) in Virginia. His Redskins are one of the more successful franchises; their stadium has been sold out for over 20 years, and the waiting list for season tickets would take over 300 years to fill. They won Super Bowl XVII, following the 1982 players' strike, and are in first place in their division following this year's strike.

Seated to the left of Cooke is Dan Rooney, president of his father Art Rooney's Pittsburgh Steelers, chairman of the League's Expansion Committee, and a member of the Management Council's Executive Committee. The eldest of Art's five sons, Dan was born the same year as the Steelers (1933). He grew up with the team, and took over as president in 1965. Dan is very highly respected by his colleagues, both because he is known as a level-headed, cleancut businessman, and because he is the leading spokesman for the 'Old Guard'.

The Old Guard was a powerful faction of owners who were members of the NFL prior to the Rozelle era. It was the keeper of the League's tradition, and the foundation upon which Rozelle's 'League Think' was built. It included Bert Bell and Tim Mara (New York Giants), George Preston Marshall (Washington Redskins), George S. Halas (Chicago Bears), and Dan's father, Arthur S. Rooney, Sr. Today, Art Rooney is the last living saint of the Old Guard, and is highly revered throughout the League. In fact, he is described as 'the most beloved figure in all of professional football'. Some of this reverence has overlapped on to Dan, increasing his influence inside the League.

Facing Rooney on the opposite side of the table is William Clay Ford, owner of the Detroit Lions, heir to the Ford Motor Company fortune (he's worth about $900 million), and a member of the Management Council's Executive Committee. One of the quieter forces in the NFL, Ford until recently never attended League meetings and was inactive in practically all NFL affairs. But he has significant experience in dealing with workers' unions, and proved an invaluable asset in management's victory over the players.

To Ford's right is Joe Robbie, owner of the Miami Dolphins, and the new $106 million, 75,000-seat 'Joe Robbie Stadium' in Dade County, Florida. Because of his recent personal investment in the construction of his football stadium, Joe was thought to be one of the owners most vulnerable to the losses incurred by a strike.

After feuding with the city of Miami for several years over the rent, and much-needed improvements on the 50-year-old Orange Bowl, Robbie packed his team's equipment bags and moved 14 miles north to 160 acres of prime land, near the junction of several main expressways and highways. He sold leases on the stadium's 216 skyboxes (called 'executive suites') for advance collateral, and raised the remaining $90 million using the Dolphins and just about everything else he owns as collateral. The repayment of loans is based on football ticket sales. A lengthy strike would have cut into those receipts drastically. But Joe came out of the whole situation practically unscathed. The players' strike was relatively short-lived, and the replacement games provided him with at least some of his required weekly income.

Still, he maintains the reputation as the cheapest man in the League. According to *Sports Illustrated* magazine, he was 'the poorest man to obtain a sports franchise in the last 20 years'. According to sports author David Harris, 'His employees describe him as someone who counts paper clips and hardly ever signs checks promptly, if at all. Hook-nosed and squat, with thick-framed glasses, Robbie has none of the glamour usually associated with the NFL, nor any of the flash traditionally associated with Miami.' Within the League, he is not particularly popular. In fact, one NFL executive said that if

87

someone killed Joe Robbie, the list of suspects would be the Miami phonebook.

Seated across the table from Robbie (and a safe distance from Commissioner Rozelle) is Allen R. Davis. As general managing partner of the (former) Oakland (now) Los Angeles (future) Irwindale Raiders (where the hell is Irwindale?), it often appears that Davis's only purpose in life is to win. Always, at any cost, he must win. One of the less censorious nicknames given to him is Al 'Just Win Baby' Davis. It also appears that he's always involved in one fight or another. If the NFL were the popular TV soap opera 'Dallas', Al Davis would be J. R. Ewing. Always looking for the edge, 'Davis acts like he's got some kind of secret information nobody else knows about,' says a former colleague, 'and much of the time it's true'.

Al is the problem child of the NFL family. He has not been a happy camper for a very long time. You see, early in 1966, the National Football League and the rival American Football League were engaged in heated battle – bidding for players, raiding each other's teams – and Al Davis, the newly elected AFL commissioner, was responsible for raiding the NFL's top quarterbacks, signing them to record-setting contracts. By the beginning of June, he had seven of their top 14 passers prepared to switch leagues and join him. Then, on 8 June, Rozelle announced that the two leagues had agreed to merge. One of the people from whom much of the negotiations leading to that announcement had been kept secret was Davis – and Al was displeased, to put it mildly. And, when Rozelle was selected over Davis to be commissioner of the merged league, Al felt hurt – at least. At most, he hates Pete's guts, and the feeling is mutual. The two have been at each other's throats for years.

Their fiercest battle to date was over Al's right to move the Raiders from Oakland to Los Angeles. After squabbling with the Oakland Coliseum Commission for a few years about improvements, including the addition of luxury 'skysuites', Al decided that the grass was greener down south. So, he announced that the Raiders would be moving into the Los Angeles Coliseum – recently vacated by the Rams, who had moved 35 miles southeast to Anaheim – to begin the 1980 season. Trouble was, the rules of the League say that a franchise transfer has to be approved by a majority of the owners. Al didn't ask for League approval, and then took on Pete Rozelle and the NFL in court when they tried to block the move. Al won that battle, to the tune of over $30 million. Pete has been lobbying Congress ever since for an antitrust exemption; preferably, a retroactive one that would force Al and his disliked Raiders back to Oakland. Then, to make matters even worse, the Raiders won the Super Bowl in 1981, following their move to Los Angeles. 'With 100 million Americans watching, Commissioner Pete Rozelle put on his best smile and gave Al Davis his second Super Bowl trophy. Davis took it, mumbling 'Thanks very much'. Despite Gene Upshaw's prediction, there was no booing from the Raiders players. Instead, most of them raised cameras and snapped away, recording forever the day they stuck it to the commissioner.'

To the left of Mr Davis is Eugene Upshaw, executive director of the NFL Players' Association. A former offensive lineman with the Oakland Raiders, Gene has moved up through the ranks of the union's internal politics to become one of the most important sports executives in America. But, as he led the players in their 1987 strike against management, he became the target of merciless criticism as a result of the super-efficient propaganda machine that the NFL has developed over the years. His leadership was constantly questioned in the media, though he maintains the respect and support of the rank-and-file. Gene is angry and frustrated. He feels that he and the executive committee of the players' union made every effort in good faith to negotiate a fair collective bargaining agreement with management. When that failed, he ordered the players back to work without an agreement and filed an antitrust lawsuit against the owners. Now he is keenly aware of the tension in the room; of the anxiety amongst the owners as they anticipate another battle in the federal courts. Gene doesn't particularly want to be here today. It's too late to bargain. He wants his day in court.

Seated opposite Upshaw is Jack Donlan, Executive Director of the NFL Management Council, and chief negotiator for the owners. Jack came into the league in 1980, after working for 15 years with the unions of National Airlines (which, by the way, no longer exists). When the council was created as a separate bargaining arm for the owners – the intent being to put distance between the players and the League – Donlan was selected to head it. He is described as very arrogant; a 'take-no-prisoners' type of negotiator; 'the owners' hired gun'. Many players consider him just downright mean, and 'an enemy of the working man'.

Ironically, Jack and Gene have grown to be friends since 1982, when Jack negotiated the last agreement, and Gene was president of the players' union. After the '82 strike, there were bitter, hostile feelings between them; they considered each other 'the enemy'. That changed over the years and, now, Gene buys gifts for Jack's daughter, and Jack was a guest at Gene's 1986 wedding. They seem to believe that their relationship will survive this difficult test. They made it through the strike OK; next, they have to make it through the courts.

On Donlan's right is Dick Berthelsen, general counsel for the Players' Association. Tall and handsome, Berthelsen graduated with honours from the University of Wisconsin Law School in 1969. After practising in Madison for three years, he was hired in the early 1970s to be assistant to the executive director of the NFLPA. He was appointed general counsel in 1983. Dick is the strong, silent type. He doesn't say much, and, when he does speak, it's in a smooth, easy-going manner. But he's got a knowledge and understanding of the law, particularly in the field of industrial relations, that is second to none. He also takes a *lot* of notes.

Opposite Berthelsen is Mick Luckhurst, seventh-year place-kicker for the Atlanta Falcons, player representative, and member of the union's executive committee. Originally from England, Mick has developed a considerable interest in American politics. In some areas, he's still just a bit naive, but he sincerely believes that the democratic system works. Apparently, he has got hold of some old 'Superman' reruns. His favourite catch-phrase for the last four weeks has been 'Truth, justice, and the American way'.

To the left of Luckhurst is Todd Christensen, ninth-year tight end for the Oakland/Los Angeles/Irwindale Raiders. Todd is an alternate player representative, and, throughout the strike, was one of the union's most vocal, if not militant members. He hurled some unquotables at strikebreakers that received national press.

Seated at the end of the table directly opposite Pete Rozelle is Roy Firestone, sports commentator and television personality. With Dick Berthelsen on his left, and Todd Christensen on his right, Firestone seems to be a hybrid of the two. His views often lean to the left, yet his delivery is quite conservative, and very polished. Roy does not rant and rave, though he does tend to go on a bit. So, as a condition of his being allowed to participate in this meeting, he was asked by the commissioner to confine his remarks to five minutes at a time.

Practically everyone in the room is talking, except Georgia Frontiere, who is meticulously checking her hair in the 8 × 10″ mirror she carries in her briefcase. Though all the media people are supposed to be 17 floors down in the hotel lobby, Georgia is sure she saw one of those pesky little jerks hanging around the ice machine near the elevator. She wants to be certain that, in case there's a camera lurking nearby, she doesn't get caught looking less than 'just so'. And Al Davis is leaning back in his chair, arms folded, looking suspiciously around the room. He appears unaware that he has begun to lean closer and closer toward Gene Upshaw.

Joe Robbie is mumbling something about gross ticket sales and loan payments. He's been having nightmarish visions of his office furniture being repossessed.

Gene and Mick are trying to calm Todd Christensen, who has begun setting little fires in the ashtrays, using ripped-up pages from management's last proposal.

Commissioner Rozelle is surveying the room. He's not looking forward to this meeting, but he knows it's something he has to do. He rises from his chair, glances over his left shoulder at the exit, then raps three times on a three-inch square of wood with the gavel his wife Carrie gave him on April Fool's Day several years ago.

Rozelle: Alright gentlemen, and you too Georgia, let's come to order. [Raps three more times.] Come on, guys! Order! Order! Here, pass this pitcher of water down to Mr Christensen, please. Thank you. [Raps three more times.] Alright, let's settle down.

I called this meeting to see if we can't work out some sort of reasonable arrangement that we can all live with. We've got to nip this war in the bud, before it destroys us all. Now, the players are back from their strike, and Gene, we're all glad about that. What we want to do now. . . .

Christensen: [Slightly louder than a whisper] What they want to do is squirm their way out of court.

Rozelle: What we want to do now is try and settle this thing between us. We don't need to bring the courts into it.

Upshaw: Hey Pete, where were you in September when we were trying to talk to these clowns?

Rozelle: Well, Gene, you know I had to maintain a certain neutrality. I didn't want to project myself as a potential hero. I couldn't very well be a mediator, since I'm employed by the 28 owners. But I thought that by bringing the parties together now, and adding the views of an objective observer, like Mr Firestone there, that we might at least get close to an agreement.

Upshaw: How can you expect to accomplish anything? Their proposal is ridiculous. We've tried bargaining, we've been on strike. Now we'll let the courts decide.

Rozelle: Well, Gene. . . .

Berthelsen: You know, Mr Commissioner, one would have thought that the owners would much prefer to keep the matter at the bargaining table. But they have pressed very hard, and the consequence of that is they've ended up back in court, exactly the place they were about 12 years ago in the Mackey suit. I wonder whether the owners won't now rethink their bargaining position and perhaps become more conciliatory.

Schramm: What the hell is *he* talking about?!!! This is war!!!

Rozelle: Tex, please. Mr Berthelsen, I can see your point. Perhaps you're right. Perhaps the owners would be willing to come back to the bargaining table. What do you think, Mr Culverhouse?

Culverhouse: I think they're full of shit. I think . . .

Rozelle: Uhhh . . . Alright. Alright. Mr Firestone, you wanted to say something?

Firestone: Yes. Thank you, Mr Commissioner. [Leans back in his chair, props an elbow on each chair arm, and clasps his hands together in front of him.] Well, the 24-day NFL strike is now officially over . . .

[Rozelle thinks to himself, 'Uh oh. He's getting wound up.'] If it had been a fight, they would have stopped it. If it had been a horse, they would have shot it. In the football vernacular, the owners' win over the players was a 'blowout', a 'rout', a 'laughter'. Only no one should be laughing. The grim reality is, the owners' arrogance and the players' collective ignorance did more than just disrupt pro football for a month. It may have left an indelible negative image for other work-force/management relationships in other industries in this country as well. . . .

[Georgia fluffs her hair and says, 'Oh come now, Roy!']
Harry Carson of the Giants said that the strike may be over, but the bitterness will linger. The entire NFL season will be marked with an asterisk; a kind of scarlet letter proclaiming failure and futility. [Leans forward, hands still clasped, placing both elbows on the table and resting his chin on his outstret-ched thumbs.] The owners, smug in their victory, in not allow-ing the striking players to play this past weekend, seem to enjoy pouring it on. That's running up the score. On the field, that's bad form. But in business, particularly in a business that operates under an illegal monopoly, it is standard fare.

Robbie: Now just one minute, young fella. First of all, I don't equate Gene Upshaw and the players' union, with their aver-age salary of $230,000, with the American blue-collar work-force. I think it's an altogether different situation. And, as for being smug, who the hell is smug?! I just had the biggest gate in the history of pro football wiped out Sunday! It seems to me just wilful destruction to wipe out a game like that!

Christensen: Hey Robbie! Why don't you shut up and let him finish!

Rozelle: Mr Christensen, please. Mr Firestone, are you finish-ed?

Firestone: No, sir.

Rozelle: [Softly] I was afraid of that. [Louder] Go on, please.

Firestone: Thank you. As I was saying, the owners never considered a conciliatory posture towards the players. They didn't *have* to, because they held all the aces, and there wasn't a joker in the deck.

Ford: Damn right!

Firestone: The players, to their discredit, never really applied sound strategy. Now, it is 'Monday morning quarterback' hind-sight, to be sure, but had the owners not been able to imple-ment replacement games, which actually turned a profit in most cases, and had the players staged a work slowdown, say, or a gradual work stoppage, perhaps the owners may not have had the upper hand. None of this had to come to pass anyway, since the eventual last-resort option – to sue the League over antitrust violations – seems to be the wisest and least damaging to the rank and file. And, by the way, that strategy could have been initiated *last August* . . .

[Rozelle looks a little anxious; checks his watch.]

Instead, about 1,500 players lost a quarter of a season's salary, not to mention incentive bonuses and postseason revenues, in what amounted to a lost cause.

Rozelle: Thank you, Mr Firestone, for your input. Yes, Mr Luckhurst?

Luckhurst: Roy is right. In retrospect, I'd rethink our strategy. First, I'd realise that fairness isn't at play when you negotiate with the NFL Management Council. I think in the back of your mind you always hope that there's going to be good-faith bargaining, and fairness, and not cheating and lying. And sadly, there was a lot of cheating and lying and misinformation involved in negotiating with the NFL Management Council. The principal piece of misinformation was that the wrong guys had the white hats on. We stood up for truth and justice and the American way and, sadly, we have now been portrayed as the black-hatted guys in the westerns. We went out for what we felt was right. We gave up a tremendous amount, and I think the players in the NFL should be proclaimed the people who stood up for truth and justice, not the bad guys.

Rozelle: Thank you, Mr Luckhurst. Uh, Mr Christensen, I realise that you are still a bit upset over the outcome of the strike, but the smoke from those fires you're setting is beginning to bother some of us. So would you please . . .

[Todd mumbles at the last few pages of management's proposal, 'This shit is a despicable crime against nature!']

Berthelsen: By the way, Mr Commissioner, Mr Schramm, everyone is aware of the coercion that went on in Texas and other places. You should know that NFL players who were illegally threatened by management to cross picket lines could go to court and seek free agency because their contract has been breached.

Rozelle: Now gentlemen, all this talk of court is just what we're trying to get away from here. Can't we seek some sort of solution among us?

Schramm: We've reiterated our position and they've reiterated their desire to have change. But I think we have made it clear that we are not giving up our structure.

Rozelle: [Whispering loudly from the left side of his mouth] Tex, we don't want to give them grounds to take us back to court!!

Donlan: Mr Commissioner, I really believe that they have to substantially reassess their positions. I think that they have over-committed or over-reached on any number of positions. We're at a roadblock. We're mired down, there isn't any question about that. But I haven't lost faith in the process.

Luckhurst: It's time for *both* sides to negotiate. But I still believe that truth and justice and the American way is going to win in the long run. And the players will get their just deserts in the end.

Upshaw: You know, it's become OK for management to try to bust a union. The entire labour movement has been suffering, and management feels it has an upper hand and can force concessions. Management seems to be on the upswing, but the pendulum always swings back. We realise that we're not dealing with the easiest group of people in the world. The NFL owners are a very cohesive group, and they're powerful and rich. That makes it more difficult. But we're not going to stand around and let management force something down our throats.

Culverhouse: Drop your free agency demand. You'll never get it. We are willing to go back to the table when free agency is no longer an issue.

Christensen: Bullshit, Mr Management Council Executive Committee chairman! We were willing to bend on that issue if the owners would come up with something solid in the way of pensions and benefits. But when our negotiating committee tried to address these important issues, you *kept* them on free agency! And then, after you finally did get around to discussing other things, you came out and told the press that there was no movement because all that was discussed was free agency. So, what's the deal? Why couldn't you guys stop jumping back and forth and just negotiate in good faith? That's the one thing I *still* cannot understand. When you look at an organisation that is as respected, and as powerful financially and politically, as the NFL, why did they not want to deal with the players? Why? We have a very healthy enterprise here!

95

Davis: I told you that not all owners are the brightest of human beings. I've told many of them in no uncertain terms that they are not men.

Upshaw: They told us, as far as free agency is concerned, that if it was 30 years, they would not give one guy freedom. Management really left us no choice but to file the lawsuit.

Rooney: For me, that lawsuit came not as a surprise, but more as a disappointment that we didn't reach agreement.

Donlan: You're damn right it wasn't a surprise! If you look at that lawsuit, it's 38 pages long. And it's very technical. You know they didn't just bang that out in a couple of hours. That baby's been on the shelf for a while, ready to go.

Luckhurst: Well of course it has, Mr Donlan. We could have *started* with the lawsuit, but the players didn't want it to go to the courts. They realise that they've won every time they've gone to court, but we thought that there would be some fair bargaining before all this came about, and there wasn't. And sadly, now, we're in court. Hopefully, we'll win and the system will change.

Georgia: Don't count on it, bucko.

Rozelle: Once again, gentlemen, I must wonder if there isn't some other solution to this problem besides litigation. Our basic problems are still there, and they're still internal. As for that elusive solution, your guess would be as good as mine. I just don't know. I do know that before we leave here, we have got to agree on *something*. If we're not careful, we could further damage our image; this time more seriously; maybe irrevocably. There is already a strong public view that professional football is more business than sport. That can only hurt the game. So please, let's proceed – cautiously – towards some sort of unity. When you have unity and harmony and can move basically as one, you can have a successful sports league.

Christensen: That all sounds very good. Very good, Pete. And I'm sure that to the eight of you [points to Rozelle and all the owners except Al Davis] it means something. But let us not forget what has happened here. Not just the strike itself, but the aftermath. The owners have played hardball since the whole process began. It's everyone's opinion that they were out all along to bust the union; humble the players somewhat. You build long-term resentment and bitterness if one side kicks the other while it's down. The owners might have won today, but if they extract too much blood, the players will win tomorrow.

Upshaw: Yeah, they definitely took a hunk of flesh out of us, but we're not busted. We're still here. We'll go before the courts. We'll let the courts decide.

Rozelle: Damn it, Gene! There you go again with the courts. Let's talk about something else – please!!!

Upshaw: Do you have a suggestion, Pete? How would *you* have us settle this thing? When we gave the collective bargaining process a chance, they refused to bargain with us by telling us that under no circumstances would they change; that we didn't have the right to be at the table; that we had no right as players to demand certain changes in the system. So why *not* court? A judge could decide the issues.

Rozelle: Well, what about arbitration? Have you thought of arbitration?

Upshaw: Yes, Pete. We suggested it. The owners turned it down flat. Isn't that right, Mr Vice-Commissioner?

Schramm: I have no comment other than it would not be acceptable to the Cowboys. We're not going to turn our system over to an arbitrator. Any time a sports dispute has been submitted to an arbitrator, the owners have lost!

Donlan: It's very simple. They want binding arbitration, and we don't want any part of it. We told Gene many, many times that we're not interested.

Upshaw: Well, do either of *you* have a suggestion?

Schramm: There's too much ground to cover to get it done in a day.

Donlan: Give us 30 days and we can work all this stuff out. I'm concentrating on just one thing and that's getting a settlement.

Upshaw: You know, I think it's rater late to be talking about collective bargaining. We will go to court.

Rozelle: Wait, Gene, wait. Let's see if *anyone* else present has something positive to contribute. Mr Cooke?

Cooke: I'm just so excited that my guys are back! This is our year, you know! We're in for some exciting football at RFK Stadium! We win the Super Bowl in a strike season! We did it before! We'll do it . . .

Rozelle: OK. OK. Thank you, Mr Cooke. Mrs Frontiere?

Georgia: [Glances at Culverhouse, who nods cautiously, indicating she may speak] Well guys, I think we should agree on half of the players' proposal, and half of our proposal, and get on with this business . . . uh . . . sport of football.

Rozelle: Right. Uh, thanks Mrs Frontiere. That's very interesting. How about you, Mr Davis? Do you have anything *constructive* to suggest?

Davis: Look fellas, I have nothing to say.

Rozelle: Great. Yes, Mr Ford?

Ford: Well, the things that were on the table before the strike are still on the table. I think that despite the suit, we can still try to work out an agreement.

Christensen: You *can't* be serious! This is not a surrender; it's a ceasefire while we proceed in another direction!

Luckhurst: It would be nice if someone could wave a magic wand and everything would be fine. But there are just too many bitter feelings that have come out of this. It'll take some time. And we will continue to stand up for truth and justice and the American way, and . . .

Rozelle: Thank you. Thank you Mick. We appreciate your input. Mr Robbie, you'd like to say something?

Robbie: Actually, I really don't care what they do. I took a big gamble on my new stadium. And now I can't relax for a minute. I have to sell that place out to help build my financial cushion. So when these players wake up and face the facts that they are over-paid, over-pampered, expendable employees who had better count their blessings and stop demanding more of our money, when that happens, let me know.

Rozelle: OK. Fine. Mr Rooney, what do you think?

Rooney: I think the strike was a theatre of the absurd, in which nobody has won and everybody has lost. Unfortunately, I don't think anyone's going to lay off their lawyer right now. We've got our work cut out for us.

Culverhouse: Frankly, I don't think the rank-and-file players know all of the issues. I know a lot of the owners don't. It seems the players believe this dispute can be settled at the negotiating table. Just drop the free agency demand. We will never allow it.

Berthelsen: Gentlemen, and Mrs Frontiere, it's very obvious to me that we are getting nowhere here. So may I interject one last thought for you to toss around in your heads. The time has come for the high court to take this issue. We've had a lot of litigation in all sports, not just football. And the issue is really whether the antitrust laws are going to dominate or whether the industrial law exemption is going to dominate, and those are two different bodies of law, actuated by different federal principles. It is now time that the issue be resolved one way or another. There is a real question of how much and to what extent football is governed by the antitrust laws. The courts have come out differently on that point. And one of the reasons this lawsuit was filed is because there's enormous uncertainty on that crucial point.

You should also know that we are seeking an injunction in our suit, meaning there would be no restrictions on veteran free agents when their contracts were up. Any player whose contract is over by 1 February 1988 would be totally free.

Upshaw: Mr Berthelsen is absolutely correct. This is getting us nowhere because these guys won't lay the facts down in front. The real facts are that we have doubled their income. They are now making $875 million in gross revenue, which is a lot of money. We're not getting as much as they're getting out of this deal. We're the ones who are taking the risks. We're getting hurt. Ours are the careers that are cut short; we have the families to support. The players come and go. They told us that at the bargaining table. But they're the stewards of the game; they actually run the game, and we're transient. I always said I guess we're the cattle and they're the ranchers. And they can always get more cattle. [Gathers his papers and rises from his chair.] I've had enough of this. See you in court.

[Upshaw turns and walks slowly past the backs of Al Davis, Dan Rooney, J. K. Cooke, and Tex Schramm. He hesitates briefly, glances at Commissioner Rozelle, then walks out of the door. A low hum falls over the room as his 6'5" figure disappears through the doorway. Pete raps weakly on his square block of wood with his gavel.]

Rozelle: Well, I guess that about says it. Somehow I knew this was going to end up an exercise in futility. So unless anybody can pull a last-minute rabbit out of a hat, it looks like we're back in court to stay. [Rozelle rises from his chair and looks at the faces around the table one more time. Once again, the tired, haggard look in his face is evident.] Well, alright then [looking into the eyes of each owner except Al Davis], I hope you're all ready for what's ahead. [Raps one last time with his gavel.] This meeting is adjourned. Thank you all for attending.

Pete turns quickly to his left and walks out of the door. Tex and Hugh, both stone-faced, leave just as quickly. Georgia, anticipating the photographers she imagines hound her constantly, again removes the 8 × 10″ mirror from her briefcase. As she touches up her lipstick, she notices that everyone except Jack Kent Cooke and Joe Robbie has gone from the room. The two men, apparently concerned about each other's hearing, are discussing, rather loudly, the merits of building one's own personal football stadium, as opposed to holding a city hostage for improvements on an old one.

Chapter Ten

By Week Six of the National Football League's 1987 regular season, the course of its future was questionable at best. The players' strike was over, but some very deep scars remained.

The players called off their strike in time to participate in the games scheduled for 18 and 19 October, but management refused to pay them, or let them play. 'They came back too late,' said Pittsburgh Steelers owner Dan Rooney. 'They missed the 14 October deadline we had set.' NBC Newscaster (and former football player) Bryant Gumble put it a bit more candidly: 'To make the players' humiliation complete, the owners have shown their total disdain for the players and fans alike, and locked the regulars out for this weekend's games.' 'If they were really interested in putting the best guys on the field and playing the best football game possible,' said New Orleans Saints offensive tackle Stan Brock, 'then 24 hours wouldn't make that much difference.' 'I foresee a very bad situation brewing,' said New York Giants team captain Harry Carson. 'I foresee players coming back with huge chips on their shoulders against everybody. I think it's everybody's opinion they tried to bust the union. Some people are very, very bitter; not just here but across the League.'

The big question was whether those bitter feelings would spill over on to the playing field; some replacement players performed well enough to warrant a closer look, and were still around when the regulars returned. The answer soon became evident. In New Orleans, striking quarterback Bobby Hebert threatened to avoid throwing passes to wide receiver Eric Martin, who had crossed the picket line. In Foxboro, Massachusetts, New England Patriots coach Raymond Berry wrote a memo that was posted at Sullivan Stadium, telling regular players that he did not want them coming into the part of the building where he was preparing the non-union team to play Houston. (I wonder where *his* loyalties lay?) But in Philadelphia, the Eagles moved their replacement players into another locker to make room for the returning regulars. When the Atlanta Falcons returned to their training facility, were turned away, and walked back out, some players from the replacement team standing on a balcony, chanted: 'One more check, baby. One more check.' And in Buffalo, at least two of the remaining replacement players found spray cans in their lockers labelled 'SCAB GUARD: KILLS GERMS ON CONTACT'. Bills quarterback Jim Kelly suggested that some of his team's veterans might not be willing to forgive strike-breakers.

The *Los Angeles Herald Examiner* reported: 'The lowest prediction is that about 100 of the striking players will lose their jobs over the next few weeks. They'll be discarded because management has found someone cheaper. It happens every summer when teams decide to cut a third-year player merely because he's about to qualify for the $40,000 jump in severance pay and full pension. Another fun-filled week or two lies ahead. In some locker rooms, winning will ease the tensions. But, regardless, the strike story hasn't been closed.'

The third and final 'ScabBall' games were played on 18 and 19 October, three days after the regular NFL players ended their work stoppage. For the true-blue, loyal National Football League fan, the end came not a moment too soon. Sportswriter John Czarnecki minced no words and spoke for many of us in his appraisal of the replacement games in general, and the Raiders/Falcons game in particular: 'The final chapter of replacement football, which began as a slam-drunk mockery of NFL credibility, ended with a contest better suited for a Monty Python skit than the Hall of Fame archives. This was silly, goofy football; it had so many bizarre plays that a viewer fully expected after another pratfall to recognise comedian Chevy Chase under a helmet. The final wrap . . . was a comedy of errors that included: formations where players headed in opposite directions, Canadian Football League-style; touchdowns nullified by penalties; fumbles and interceptions galore; offensive linemen tackling pass rushers; and mistakes, mental and physical, so plentiful that with eight minutes left in the game, neither team had a timeout remaining. Call it mismanaged confusion.'

And by the end of Week Six (actually, it was Week Five; remember, the Week Three games were cancelled), 'confusion' was a pretty apt description of the NFL standings. In the American Football Conference (AFC; a 'conference' is a division of the League), the Miami Dolphins, Kansas City Chiefs and Cincinnati Bengals – all former Super Bowl teams – occupied the basements of their respective divisions. In the AFC Central division, there was a three-way tie for first place between the Houston Oilers, Cleveland Browns and Pittsburgh Steelers (there are only four teams in the division); and in the AFC East, there was a three-way tie for last place between the Buffalo Bills, Indianapolis Colts and Miami Dolphins (there are five teams in that division). Over in the National Football Conference (NFC), things were pretty much status quo, with two glaring exceptions: the New York Giants and the New Orleans Saints.

The NFC has been the stronger of the two conferences in the '80s; it has won five of the eight Super Bowls. At the end of 'StrikeBall '87' most of its principals were leading their divisions as usual – the San Francisco 49ers in the NFC West, the Chicago Bears in the NFC Central, and the Dallas Cowboys and Washington Redskins neck-and-neck in the NFC East. But the New York Giants, the defending Super Bowl Champions, had not won a *single* game! Said linebacker Harry Carson of his 0 and 5 team: 'You're either going to see a very good football team go down the drain, or you're going to see one of the greatest comebacks of all time.' And even more surprising than that was the sudden (after 21 years) emergence of the New Orleans Saints. Their 3 and 2 record was the best start they'd had in a while; but beyond that, they were playing with a certain confidence, heretofore absent from their club. When the Saints came on to the field, it was obvious that they believed they could win. And each time they did, the owner, auto dealer Tom Benson, grabbed a black parasol with a gold fringe (Saints colours) and pranced up and down the sideline, twisting and turning, waving and throwing kisses to the crowd. The dance became known as the 'Benson Boogie', and Mr Benson got to do it 12 times in 1987.

After Week Six, teams began trimming their rosters. The League allowed each club to retain an 85-man roster (maximum 40 replacements, plus the 45 regulars), but they could only activate 45 for Week Seven games. The Vikings kept only one replacement player, defensive lineman Stafford Mays.

The Seattle Seahawks kept two, quarterback Bruch Mathison and running back Eric Lane. The 49ers kept 14 strikebreakers, the Raiders kept 17, and the Chargers kept 19. The Cowboys kept 26 replacements, and the Houston Oilers retained the maximum 40. Said 49ers coach Bill Walsh, 'Only a paranoid organisation would keep the 85 players allowed. There are some very suspicious owners or paranoid people who say that the regular players will walk out again, and we'll be ready if they do. But that's absolute overkill.' In Chicago, head coach Mike Ditka allowed the regular players to decide whether to keep any of the replacements around. The vote was 44-1 in favour of dumping them all. But then Ditka had second thoughts. So he told his team that *he* was the boss, and *he* would make that decision. He kept 19 strikebreakers. All rosters would be cut again for Week Eight, dropping the player limit from 85 to 55 – 45 active and a ten-man reserve squad. The rest of the season would be played with the normal 50-man squad – 45 active and five reserves.

Preparations around the League for the Week Seven games were filled with tension and anxiety; it was the time when regular players and the remaining strikebreakers were forced to work together. In some places, the wounds from the strike seemed to begin to heal. But in other camps, recapturing the pre-strike atmosphere was a bit more dfficult. The returning Los Angeles Raiders were joined on the practice field by the 13 veterans who'd crossed the picket line, and the ten remaining replacement players. You could cut the tension in the air with a knife. 'No one has said anything,' said wide receiver Mervyn Fernandez, who crossed the picket line one day before the strike ended, 'but I can tell by people's attitudes who's feeling a little resentment and who's not. It's more of a work ethic around here now than before the strike. There is not so much joking around. Most people are pretty quiet and in their own circles. But I think we'll break out of that in a short time. I think the closer we get to the game, the more we'll loosen up and become a team.'

Linebacker Rod Martin, a team captain, a hardline union member, and a distant cousin of mine, was unmistakably . . . shall we say, *displeased* . . . upon his return to work. He said he felt like a player without a team: 'First of all, they had us dressing in the cafeteria while the replacements were still occupying our cubicles. Then to hear we couldn't come back and play that weekend's game – I thought that was another slap on the wrist for doing what we felt was right as individuals, for standing up for a principle. It was just a down situation. I think it's going to take maybe a week or two. We're all still in a little funk. You could definitely feel the thickness in the air. But we had a meeting, and I said, as a captain, "Put your feelings aside. We're here to win football games. We're all a team now so we've got to work together."''

Seahawks quarterback Bruce Mathison, one of two replacement players retained in Seattle, said that his reception by the returning regulars was extremely cold. 'Nothing was said at all. I have talked more at a funeral. Of course, it could have been worse. There could have been eggs, rocks, all kinds of junk in my helmet. It got a little better once practice started.'

The Week Seven games heralded the return of the regular NFL players, and, in general, the return to business as usual. Chicago Bears quarterback Jim McMahon, who had suffered a career threatening shoulder injury and had surgery in the offseason, returned to the lineup in the second half of their first post-strike game, and led his team to a 27–26 victory over the Tampa Bay Buccaneers.

The New York Giants got their first victory of the season in a convincing 30–7 thrashing of the St Louis Cardinals. Facing the improbable task of winning their final ten games to make the playoffs, the Giants improved their record to one win and five losses. Quarterback Phil Simms set a team record with his 80.95 per cent passing efficiency; he completed 17 of 21 passes, gaining 253 yards. And the defence did a vintage job, forcing four turnovers, two of which turned into Giants touchdowns. The Giants gave the impression that they just might be able to come out of the hole they'd dug for themselves. 'We're not in a hole,' said Harry Carson, 'we're in a canyon.'

In the contest between the San Francisco 49ers and New Orleans Saints, business as usual was defined as 'opportunistic offence and tough defence from San Francisco, self-destructive errors by New Orleans'. The Saints lost 83 yards due to penalties; the 49ers got five first-downs as a result. After the 24–22 victory, San Francisco improved its record to 5 and 1.

The returning Washington Redskins endured the wrath of their fans for over 50 minutes of their game against the New

York Jets. They were down 16–7 wih just under six minutes remaining, when many in the sellout crowd of 53,497 began shouting, 'Bring back the scabs.' (Theirs was one of only three replacement teams to go 3 and 0 during the strike.) But they rallied at the end of the game, scoring ten points in the final six minutes, and winning 17–16. Sports analyst Pete Axthelm said one week after the strike ended: 'Washington was the biggest winner in the NFL strike. They won every game with their scab team, and the veterans came back united. They'll win the Super Bowl.'

By the end of Week Seven, there was very little mention of the strike that put an asterisk beside the 1987 NFL season. Except for some occasional booing by fans who were still angry at the players for the disruption of the season, it appeared to be almost forgotten. Game attendance figures increased dramatically (not to the pre-strike highs, but certainly far beyond the strike numbers), and TV ratings were on the way back up.

Meanwhile, the League's rebates to the networks for lost advertising revenue were expected to reach $60 million, 14 per cent of the $440-million rights fee for 1987. The cancelled games of 27 September would cost the League about $21 million, which would be deducted from the networks' first payment for 1988.

On 27 October, NFL officials announced their desire to resume negotiations with the players' union. The two sides had not met since 11 October, Day 20 of the strike, when they reached agreement on just eight of the 38 contract issues. Management walked out of that meeting, the strike ended four days later, and the union filed its antitrust suit. Commissioner Rozelle expressed his hope that resumed talks would come to a successful conclusion by March 1988, so that the League could proceed with its 1989 expansion plans. But the union was not interested in returning to the bargaining table unless the owners changed their position on major issues. Said union spokesman Doug Allen, 'Things stand just where they stood when they walked away from the table. Until we see a substantive change in their position, we don't see any reason for resuming talks.'

So the season proceeded – with no collective bargaining agreement in the forseeable future.

The Saints continued their amazing march toward the playoffs with a 38–0 dismantling of the lowly Atlanta Falcons in
Week Eight, and improved their record to 4 and 3. It was the
most lopsided victory in Saints history, and came on their 21st
birthday (the NFL awarded an expansion franchise to New
Orleans on 1 November 1966 – All Saints Day). 'We had a
great game-plan and we executed it,' said New Orleans quarterback Bobby Hebert. 'It was just one of those games where
a lot of things went right for us.' But Falcons coach Marion
Campbell was abolutely livid; he even threatened to make
some personnel changes. 'I hope they get as mad as I am right
now,' he said after the embarrassing loss. 'We don't have to
worry about standings or statistics [they were 2 and 5]. These
players have to worry about their careers. I won't stand for
that kind of play.'

In Miami, Dolphins quarterback Dan Marino inched closer
and closer to an NFL passing record held by Johnny Unitas,
the all-time great quarterback for the Baltimore Colts of the
1960s. Marino, the NFL's top-rated passer, completed 25 of
31 passes against the Pittsburgh Steelers for over 300 yards
and four touchdowns. It was the 14th time in his career that
he'd thrown four touchdown passes in a game, just three shy
of Unitas's record. The Dolphins' 35–24 victory gave them a 3
and 4 record. 'It was a win we had to have,' said coach Don
Shula.

As the Dallas Cowboys prepared for their Monday night
contest against the New York Giants in Texas Stadium, they
also contemplated their 'home field disadvantage'. During the
strike, there had been well documented strife in Dallas; it's
not one of the more pro-union towns. The scab team had won
two of its three games, and the regulars had been beaten the
previous week, 37–20, by the Philadelphia Eagles. There were
rumours flying all week that superstar running back Tony
Dorsett was going to be traded to Denver (which management
vehemently denied), and general unrest throughout the organisation. The players braced for the worse. Linebacker Jeff
Rohrer, who during the strike had called Cowboys fans stupid
for being led around by their noses by management, said
they'd probably get booed Monday night. 'The fans will probably be down on us good. They'll let us have it.' Defensive
back Bill Bates said, 'The fans are supposed to be on our side.

If they boo us, I'll be ashamed. The home field advantage is supposed to be in your favour and not against you. I can't believe the true-blue fans will boo us.' Well, they did. But the mood was tempered, somewhat, by the Cowboys 33–24 victory over the hapless Giants, raising Dallas's record to 4 and 3, and dropping the Giants' record to 1 and 6. In addition to the defeat, the Giants lost quarterback Phil Simms, the Most Valuable Player (MVP) in Super Bowl XXI, after he injured his left knee in the fourth quarter of the game.

In Chicago, the topics of conversation around the Bears' camp following the games of Week Eight were, firstly, coach Mike Ditka's slurred speech on a taped TV show, and secondly, William 'The Refrigerator' Perry's weight. The 'Fridge' was tipping the scales at somewhere between 325 and 340 lbs, nowhere near the 315 maximum imposed by Coach Ditka. 'I don't want to talk about that,' was all William would say. Talking, on the other hand, had got the coach into a bit of hot water. After his team defeated the Kansas City Chiefs 31–28, improving their record to 6 and 1, Coach Ditka celebrated with a little champagne and song at a local restaurant. Then he went to tape the weekly segment of 'Bears Extra', a television talk-show. His slurred speech, sing-song delivery, and heavy eyes led viewers to believe that he was either drunk or overly tired. 'Yeah, that's it,' Ditka said afterwards, 'I really got tired. I fell asleep and just couldn't get back with it.' Uh huh.

As Week Ten approached, Bears Super Superstar running back (and all-round nice guy) Walter 'Sweetness' Payton revealed that his 13th and final season in the NFL was not shaping into a pleasant one. Before the season began, Walter had announced his plan to retire. Now he was very unhappy with the dramatic reduction of his playing time; but beyond that, he felt that the close relationships he'd had with many of his teammates were fading.

Meanwhile, Jack Donlan and Gene Upshaw were in Key Biscayne, Florida – but not for a bargaining session. They were attending an NFL retirement board meeting. Asked when contract talks would resume, Donlan said he didn't have the foggiest idea. 'Regardless of what happens in court, at some point there has to be a settlement at the bargaining table, whether it's December 1987 or December 1989.'

And speaking of court, November was (partial) pay-up time for the League, a result of one of the many antitrust lawsuits filed against it. Its attempts to block the Oakland Raiders from moving to Los Angeles had cost dearly. The award to the Raiders was sent back to a lower court for further consideration, but the Coliseum Commission and its lawyers walked away with nearly $30 million. After paying its own attorneys, the League's tab was about $40 million.

In New England, Patriots owner Billy Sullivan, always in one financial bind or another, was now faced with the probability of a hostile takeover of his team. Two stockholders, Philadelphia businessmen Fran Murray and John Carlton, decided to exercise an option to buy the Patriots that they'd obtained from Billy over a year previously. Although Sullivan said he'd changed his mind, and no longer wanted to sell, Murray's attorney Robert Popeo said, 'We have a legal and binding option to purchase the team, and we will go ahead and exercise it. Nothing is finalised yet, but we have a plan and we're putting it in motion.' The price tag on the team was $63 million, which would rise to $65 million if the option were not exercised by 31 December 1987.

At Thanksgiving, a time for doing blessings and offering thanks, the most grateful people around the National Football League had to be the lawyers for the Los Angeles Raiders. By now, the club had lawsuits, depositions, environmental studies, City Hall fights and state legislative bills coming out of its ears. You see, Big Al had grown a bit weary of Los Angeles. Actually, it was the Coliseum Commission itself with whom he was fighting. It wasn't the same Commission that had wined and dined and finally lured the Raiders to Los Angeles, with the promise of luxury suites in the Coliseum. No, no. This was the Commission with new members, who vetoed the construction of the boxes, and incurred the wrath of Al Davis. Al tried to force Commission Number Two to honour the committments of Commission Number One, but decided instead to just pack up his team (*again*) and move somewhere else (*again*). The lucky winner this time was Irwindale, California, a small town approximately 65 miles east of L.A. Or so they tell me. I'd never heard of Irwindale before the Raiders dug it up. The burning question remains: 'Where the hell is Irwindale?'

Anyway, the Raiders' legal staff's busy itinerary would

begin in December, with the taxpayers' suit filed against Irwindale by an L.A. city councillor, which sought to prevent the city from building a new stadium for the Raiders. Next, they'd be in federal court in January to hear the court's decision on how much money they'd receive from their antitrust victory over the NFL. Then comes the Irwindale environmental study to determine the feasibility and environmental impact of a new stadium on the town. Then, there's the appeal of the $2 million award (down from $10 million) given Eugene Klein in the 'medical landmark' case against Al Davis, who was accused of prompting Mr Klein's heart attack. And finally, there's the bill introduced to the California Legislature that would prevent Irwindale from building a stadium on the grounds that other priorities (the homeless, trauma centres and over-crowded schools) should come first.

Of course, Al Davis and his Raiders were not the only parties with a gripe against the League. Kelly Stouffer, an unsigned rookie quarterback, sought to intervene as a plaintiff in the NFLPA's antitrust suit against the NFL. Stouffer and the St Louis Cardinals, who had made him their first draft choice in '87, couldn't seem to come to terms on a contract; so Stouffer wanted to negotiate with other teams. But, bound by the restraints of the draft, he was of course unable to do so. In addition to his motion to intervene, he also filed a class-action suit on behalf of all potential players, seeking (like the NFLPA) to eliminate all restraints on player movement.

Meanwhile, back on the playing field, the Saints continued to prove that they were no fluke. Known, as recently as two seasons ago, as the 'New Orleans Aints' because of their poor playing, they served notice one more time that these Saints aren't the 'Aints. The Pittsburgh Steelers were victim number eight, giving New Orleans an 8 and 3 record in Week 12. By now, the playoff picture was beginning to take shape, and, for the first time in its 21-year history, the Saints were a sure bet for postseason play. The whole season may have been a bust for everyone else, but they were partying in the streets in New Orleans. 'NFL WOES WON'T SPOIL OUR PARTY' read the headline of a New Orleans sports page. While most of the media proclaimed doom and gloom and the sad state of the League after the union's ill-advised strike, the 'Crescent City' would have none of it. Just before the Saints disposed of the

Tampa Bay Buccaneers in the Week 13 game, sportswriter Dave Lagarde wrote: 'No way any experts or party-pooping periodicals are going to spoil the hellzapoppin' celebration going on in the pubs, streets, and Superdome seats of this town. Not when a team . . . normally interred in the NFL's version of a pauper's grave has risen from the dead after a 20-year nap. . . . No sir. No way. Not this year. . . . Strike, smike. This party has only just begun.'

Most of the playoff berths in the NFC were decided by Week 13. It seemed to me that no one in the AFC *wanted* to go to the playoffs. Practically every team in the conference had the same record (7 and 5). The contest would not be decided until the very last moment.

Here's how it works: each conference (NFC and AFC) is split into three divisions (East, West and Central). In each of the six divisions, the team with the best record wins the division title. Then, in each of the conferences, the *two* teams with the *next* best records go to the playoffs as the 'wild cards'. Thus, ten of the 28 teams (five from each conference) advance to postseason play. Now each conference must find a champion to send to the Super Bowl. In the first round of the playoffs, the two wild-card teams play each other. The winner advances to the next round; the loser watches the remainder of the football season on television with the rest of us. In the second round, the surviving wild-card team plays one of the division champions. The other two division champs play each other. The winners of those two games play for the conference championship, and that winning team goes to the Super Bowl. Got it?

So, by 7 December, four teams were definitely playoff bound: In the NFC East, the Washington Redskins clinched the division title with a record of nine wins and three losses, with three games remaining. The next team in that division, Dallas, had a record of 5 and 7 – no mathematical way of catching up. In the NFC Central, the Chicago Bears clinched the title with a 10 and 2 record; Minnesota, at 7 and 5, had two chances of catching the Bears – slim and none. The title in the NFC West was not yet decided, though both the San Francisco 49ers (10 and 2) and the New Orleans Saints (9 and 3) clinched a playoff spot of some sort. With three games to go, one team would be the division champion, and the other would be a wild card.

The 'Monday Night Football' contest on 14 December – Week 14 – was promoted as a mini-NFC championship. The Bears and the 49ers both came in with 10 and 2 records. This had the makings of a great game. It turned into a massacre. With both of the star quarterbacks (Jim McMahon for the Bears, and Joe Montana for the 49ers) out of the game with injuries, one would have thought that the offences, or at least the passing games, would even out. But the 49ers had other ideas. Back-up quarterback Steve Young stepped in and threw three touchdown passes to their wide receiver sensation, Jerry Rice, on the way to a 41–0 trouncing of the Bears. Coach Ditka was so incensed at the performance of his back-up quarterback, Mike Tomczak, that he could not wait until his team went into the locker room, or even until they were out of the range of TV cameras and microphones, to give the player an opinionated earful. With arms flailing and eyes bulging, he let Tomczak have it, right there on the field, on national television.

The three AFC division titles, the two AFC wild cards, and the NFC West were all decided on the final weekend of the regular season. The San Francisco 49ers won the NFC West title by completely destroying the Los Angeles Rams 48–0. Never before had a Rams team been so humbled. The 49ers, said the press, 'toyed with the Rams, as if experimenting for the betterment of football science'. The Rams finished the season with a 6 and 9 record, and the 49ers got to rest for a week before their first playoff game.

The Denver Broncos won the AFC West divisional title by beating the San Diego Chargers (with a little help from Mother Nature), 24–0. There was 14 inches of snow on the ground at game time in Denver; three more inches fell during the game. The temperature was 20°F; with the wind-chill factor, it was *minus* 23°. On one Denver punt, the Charger punt returner, Lionel James, never took his hands out of his pockets. The whole game went pretty much the same way. The Chargers, who at one point during the season had an 8 and 1 record, finished with a record of 8 wins and 7 losses.

The Seattle Seahawks lost their final game to the Kansas City Chiefs, 41–20, but still earned a wild-card berth with their 9 and 6 regular season record. The Chiefs finished with a 4 and 11 record. The Houston Oilers won the other AFC wild-card spot with a 9 and 6 record, after slipping by the Cincinnati Bengals (another 4 and 11 finisher) 21–17. The Indianapolis Colts won the AFC East title with a 9 and 6 record, and the Cleveland Browns won the AFC Central with ten wins and five losses.

The Minnesota Vikings lost their final regular season game in overtime to the Washington Redskins 27–24, and had to hope for a St Louis Cardinals loss in order to capture the final NFC wild-card spot. The Cardinals very kindly obliged by losing their final game of the season to the Cowboys 21–16, thereby dropping their record to seven wins and eight losses. Minnesota's 8 and 7 record was good enough for the wild-card berth.

The playoff picture was now complete. In the NFC, it was Washington, Chicago, San Francisco, Minnesota and New Orleans; in the AFC, it was Denver, Cleveland, Indianapolis, Houston and Seattle. The first games – the wild-card matchups – were on Sunday, 3 January 1988.

In Houston, the Oilers beat the Seahawks in overtime 23–20. And in New Orleans, the Vikings turned out the lights on the Saints' party with a 44–10 drubbing before 68,127 disappointed Saints fans. Owner Tom Benson made one final appearance on the sideline (with his parasol) and – waving to the crowd – did a sedate boogie. Oh, what a season they had had! Head coach Jim Mora was naturally disappointed, but philosophised: 'The team accomplished more things this season than anybody expected. We won a lot of games and had a lot of good things happen to us. We have nothing to be ashamed of. Lack of playoff experience wasn't a factor. We just got beaten by a better team.' The Saints' 12 and 3 regular season record was second only to San Francisco's 13 and 2.

The next round of games matched wild card Minnesota against the NFC West champion 49ers, and the wild-card Houston Oilers against the AFC West champion Denver Broncos. The NFC East and Central title-winners, the Redskins and the Browns respectively, played each other, as did the AFC East and Central champions, Indianapolis and Cleveland. The shocker of the weekend was the Vikings' upset victory over the San Francisco 49ers. Minnesota's record was the worst of the ten teams going to the playoffs (8 and 7); the 49ers' was the best in the League (13 and 2). The Vikings were decided underdogs going into San Francisco's Candle-stick Park; the 49ers were 10½ point favourites, playing at home, before 62,547 of their closest friends, after a week of rest and healing time. Well, they certainly didn't play poorly against the Vikings; they scored 24 points. The Vikings simply played better. They put constant pressure on 49ers quarter-back Joe Montana, sacking him four times, and keeping him from connecting with Jerry Rice, their best receiver. Montana was eventually benched in favour of the more agile backup, Steve Young. But it was too little, too late and the Vikings prevailed 36–24.

The Denver Broncos knocked the Houston Oilers out of con-tention with a lopsided 34–10 victory in Mile High Stadium. The Cleveland Browns disposed of the Indianapolis Colts 28–21, setting up the AFC conference championship game be-tween the Browns and the Broncos.

In the NFC, the Redskins dismissed the Bears from the play-offs with a 21–17 victory. It was the second straight year that Washington had come into Chicago's Soldier Field and beaten the Bears in the playoffs. The game-winning play came with three minutes remaining in the third quarter, and the score tied at 14. Cornerback Darrell Green did his impression of hurdler Edwin Moses when he returned a Chicago punt 52 yards for a touchdown, leaping over a defender near the goal line. Green said afterwards, 'I'd gone that far, I wanted to score. I saw him coming, so I decided to try jumping over him.' It worked; his score broke the tie, and the Bears could manage only three more points.

The loss was the last game for running back Walter 'Sweet-ness' Payton. After 13 seasons, the NFL's all-time leading rusher (16,726 yards) was hanging up his cleats. His future plans include owning an NFL franchise. He has also been assured of a position on the Bears' board of directors. 'In 13 years here, there have been a lot of good times and a lot of bad times,' Payton's formal farewell statement began. 'There have been times when I wanted to quit, and times when I couldn't see quitting in sight. The game of football has been very good to me. It doesn't owe me a thing. This team has given me an opportunity to display my talents and my ability, and I'd like to thank them for giving me the courtesy of letting me go out there. My teammates, I can't say enough about them. They're great in defeat as well as victory. I think the whole thing, the bottom line, is God's been very good to me in giving me this opportunity to play the game of football, and I've truly been blessed. Thank you.'

During the week before the Conference Championship games, St Louis Cardinals owner William Bidwill informed the League of his desire to move his team to Phoenix, Arizona before the beginning of the next season. Bidwill had been unhappy in St Louis, and shopping for a new home for the last four years. The Cardinal's field, Busch Stadium, was the second smallest in the NFL (after the Houston Astrodome) with 54,392 seats. To get League approval for the move, three-fourths of the club owners must support it. The vote was taken at the annual owners meeting in March. The Cardinals would have no problem getting approval. 'No one wants to see a franchise move,' said one owner, 'but this is no overnight move.' So, the Cardinals will open the 1988 season in the 70,491-seat Sun Devil Stadium, on the campus of Arizona State University. They will be known as the Phoenix Cardinals.

The two Super Bowl teams were decided on Sunday, 17 January. In Denver's Mile High Stadium, the Broncos and the Cleveland Browns replayed their 1987 meeting in the AFC Championship game. The game was a little different, but the outcome was the same. After trailing 21–3 at half-time, the Browns rallied to score four touchdowns in 15 minutes. With a little over five minutes remaining in the game and the score tied at 31, the Broncos regained the lead on a 20-yard pass from quarterback John Elway to running back Sammy Winder. Cleveland still had one last chance to at least score and send the game into overtime. They drove all the way to the eight-yard line but, with just over a minute left in the game, an ill-timed, ill-fated fumble by the normally sure-handed, versatile running back, Ernest Byner, ended the Browns' season. For the second time in two years, the Browns were knocked out of the Super Bowl by the Broncos. The final score was 38–31, to Denver.

In Washington's Robert F. Kennedy Stadium, the Redskins had their hands full with the 'Cinderella' Vikings. It took a little extra pressure from the much heralded Redskins defence to assure a 17–10 victory. Twice in the last quarter, they stopped a Minnesota scoring threat, first on the three-yard line, then on the one-foot line. 'It was the story of the season,' said Minnesota offensive lineman Gary Zimmerman. 'We'd get down to the goal line and not score.' But the Redskins got help from their 55,212 fans. The crowd noise made it difficult for the Vikings to hear their quarterback's audibles. 'That's why they had so many sacks,' continued Zimmerman. 'We had half the line doing one thing and half doing another.' The fact is, however, that the Redskins were bigger, stronger, and smarter that day. They were going to the Super Bowl. The Vikings were going home.

Chapter Eleven

Super Bowl XXII (I wonder why they use Roman numerals instead of just writing 22? It's not like American football was played in ancient Rome) was being staged at Jack Murphy Stadium, home of the San Diego Chargers, on 31 January 1988. The Super Bowl is actually a week-long party for NFL owners and a few thousand of their very closest friends, culminating with a football game on Sunday. The money that is generated during the week of festivities is what makes the Super Bowl the big deal that it is. Everyone wants to be a part of it; not necessarily out of any love for the game, but because only a select few people are allowed to participate. So there's a certain status attached, which some people will go to any lengths to attain.

First, the host city. Landing the Super Bowl, as with any other major event, is a guaranteed payday for the city it is held in. Hotels, restaurants, public transport, souvenir vendors, parking lots, all stand to make a ton of money. And since there are only a few cities in America that are eligible to play host, it is indeed a major coup. One of the last things Gene Klein did before he sold the Chargers and got out of the NFL was to get the Super Bowl for San Diego. The city had never been awarded the event in the past because of the size of its stadium (60,750 seats after completion of a major expansion in 1984). The league required a minimum of 70,000 seats. So, at the owners' meeting in 1984, when the 1987 and 1988 Super Bowl sites were decided, Klein lobbied hard for San Diego, offering to install 13,000 additional seats. After extended debate, San Diego won a majority vote, 16–12, over Miami and was awarded Super Bowl XXII in 1988.

Super Bowl Week is traditionally filled with activity, and San Diego was not about to be outdone. The week included countless interviews of players, coaches, wives and fans. There were over 2,100 media people. From Wednesday through Sunday there was a huge fiesta just across the Mexican border, in Tijuana's main market-place. On Thursday, the fourth annual Buick Super Bowl Golf Classic was played at the Torrey Pines Golf Course in LaJolla. More than 200 sports celebrities, journalists, and amateur golfers participated in the charity event. Proceeds went to the NFL's Dire Need Fund, which provides financial assistance to former NFL players from the pre-1959 era. On Saturday, there was another spectacular fiesta, this time in San Diego's 'Old Town', featuring ethnic entertainment, Mexican food, a re-enactment of a 19th-century military installation, and free tours through Old Town's parks and museums. The world famous San Diego Zoo had a special display of two giant black-and-white pandas from the People's Republic of China. On Saturday night, there was the NFL Alumni's Player of the Year Awards dinner, and the annual party for owners and their families. Then on Sunday morning there was a giant pep rally, co-ordinated at several local shopping malls, complete with wide-screen televisions and a simultaneous balloon release.

Then came Commissioner Rozelle's annual pre-Superbowl news conference. He made several pertinent points, among them the League's expansion plans: two teams approximately two years after a collective bargaining agreement is reached with the Players' Association. Of course, since the union and management had not met in months, and no progress had been made towards returning to the bargaining table, it's a pretty safe bet that expansion will probably be delayed a bit.

Another pressing issue that had to be addressed was all the recent attention given to the League's 68-year history of overt bigotry. The Commissioner offered a very weak excuse. 'It's been called by some a racist league. I don't like that. But with all the attention to hire black coaches and to have other businesses hire minorities, it probably is a good thing if it brings results. I guess there has been an old-boy network. Most head coaches have picked assistants they had coached with or played with as far back as high school and college.' (And, of course, there were no black players in their high schools and colleges.)

New York Times columnist Ira Berkow offered this poignant observation: 'The old-boy network, or cronyism, or racism, has, by its very nature, excluded a segment of American society from advancement simply because of the colour of its skin. . . .

Difficult to conceive, though, that with a black on the Supreme Court, and blacks in the Cabinet and Congress, and blacks in the federal judiciary, and black brain surgeons, and black astronauts, and black college professors, and blacks who head big businesses, and even black quarterbacks, one of whom is in the Super Bowl – quarterback being the ultimate "thinking" or "decision-making" position once considered the sole province of whites – that there is not, and has not been a single black man qualified to be a professional head coach, and this in a game in which the single most crucial activity is for one man to jump on top of another.'

As game day approached, the hoopla reached a fever pitch. The stars of the week-long media blitz were the opposing quarterbacks, Doug Williams of the Washington Redskins, and John Elway of the Denver Broncos. By all accounts, Elway was the National Football League's version of the second coming of the Christ. He was GREAT, he was WONDERFUL, he could do ANYTHING! He was a one-man team. The others were just along for the ride. Without him, said columnist Melvin Durslag, 'Where does Denver go for help? *Wholly* because of Elway, the bookmaker this time posts Denver a favourite by $3\frac{1}{2}$ points.' Doesn't say a lot for the rest of the Broncos team, does it?

Then there was Doug Williams, the first black quarterback to start in a Super Bowl. The question of the week was, of course, 'How does it feel to be a black quarterback in the Super Bowl?' Now, let's think about that question for just a moment. Doug has been black all of his life; yet, the question was posed as if he'd once been a *white* quarterback. Kind of silly, huh? 'The media has made it an issue,' he said. 'But I don't feel it's an issue.'

It is ironic, however, that the 'First Black Quarterback to Start in a Super Bowl' – or FBQSSB for short – should represent the organisation that was last in the League to go kicking and screaming into integration. As late as 1961, the Redskins were a lily-white team. It took coercion from President Kennedy's Secretary of the Interior to get owner George Preston Marshall to change his bigoted ways. Marshall's own greed played an important part as well. In 1961, a new stadium, almost twice the size of the one the Redskins were in, was being built on federal property. Marshall was told in no uncertain terms that, unless he integrated his football team, he would be denied use of the new stadium. Marshall agreed to comply. Still, the Redskins team that inaugurated what is now Robert F. Kennedy Stadium was still all white in 1961. In one final act of defiance, Marshall traded his 1962 first-round draft choice (which would have given him a crack at the (black) running back Ernie Davis, the Heisman Trophy winner from Syracuse University) to the Cleveland Browns in exchange for running back Bobby Mitchell. You see, Marshall was determined that he was not going to *draft* a black player. So that year, Bobby Mitchell took the field as the Redskins' first black player. As Marshall's health went into decline a few years later, and he began to fade from the scene, the Redskins became as integrated as any other team. Said Don Frederick, a political editor for a local newspaper, and a lifelong Redskins fan: 'Older Washington fans probably haven't given George Preston Marshall a thought in years. And younger fans probably have never heard of him. But for those few of us who will never forget what he stood for, the first snap Doug Williams takes on Sunday will be that much sweeter.'

That, and every bit of Super Bowl action, was broadcast worldwide over television and radio airwaves. There were over 200 representatives of ABC Television (the 'official' network of Super Bowl XXII), with an incredible array of state-of-the-art high-tech video equipment. They had 24 vehicles, over 14 miles of cables for cameras and microphones, 25 cameras – including one in a blimp, one in a helicopter, and a remote-controlled one attached to one of the goal posts – and nearly 250 TV monitors for the control trucks, the press, and the VIPs. The event was shown on 222 television stations in the US (the estimated American audience was more than 120 million people), in more than 50 foreign countries, and on all overseas US military posts. CBS Radio (the official radio station of Super Bowl XXII) preceded its live broadcast with the conclusion of the 20-part 'Road to the Super Bowl' series. The two-minute reports had been heard on CBS each weekday before the game. Following the game broadcast, there would be a one-hour talk-show featuring game highlights, interviews, and listener calls.

The game began at 3 p.m. Pacific Standard Time. The day was clear and cool. The skies were slightly overcast (it had been raining for a couple of days), but the sun managed to push itself through right around game time. The temperature was mild, in the 60s, and there was a slight breeze from the Pacific Ocean.

Washington won the coin toss and elected to receive. Redskins wide receiver Ricky Sanders caught the Denver kickoff and returned it 16 yards. The 'Skins kept the ball for just under two minutes, attempting to run it twice and throw it once, all to no avail; they had to punt. Denver took over on its own 44-yard line, and on the first play from scrimmage, scored with a 56-yard touchdown pass from John Elway to wide receiver Ricky Nattiel. The score was 7–0 after the successful point-after-touchdown (PAT). They made it look easy. On Washington's next possession, they sputtered again. Rookie running back Timmy Smith attempted to return Denver's kickoff, and gained only 15 yards. He tried three more times to run, and Doug Williams tried twice to pass, again all for naught. Something was not quite right. The Redskins seemed confused, and unable to get their game going. The defensive backs, among them some of the fastest men in the NFL, were being burned (mercilessly outrun) by the Broncos receivers, and the defence seemed incapable of containing Elway. On Denver's second possession, they drove 61 yards downfield in seven plays. Unable to run the ball in from the six-yard line, they settled for a field goal, and with just over six minutes elapsed in the first quarter, led the Redskins 10–0. That would be all the scoring the Denver Broncos would do in Super Bowl XXII because, as the first quarter wound down, the Washington Redskins readjusted themselves. And when the second quarter began, the *real* Redskins appeared – seemingly from nowhere.

Actually, they just came out in more appropriate moccasins. You see, the field was very beautiful, neatly manicured and protected; but, because of the recent rain, it was also quite slippery and loose. Many of the Broncos players had noticed it during pregame warmups, and decided to wear shoes with longer than average cleats, so they'd have better footing. Many of the Redskins players did not notice it until the first quarter, after they'd spotted Denver 10 points. 'I was slipping all over the place,' said Sanders later. 'I just couldn't get my footing. I couldn't get upfield like I wanted to.' Defensive end Charles

Mann concurred: 'It was fine in pregame, but I was slipping and sliding like crazy once the game began. You need traction when Elway's out there. He'd give a little head fake, and I'd slip and fall down.' Several Redskins switched to longer cleats after the first quarter, and the results were dramatic.

The second quarter – 'The Incredible Quarter' – began with an incomplete pass from Elway, intended for Ricky Nattiel. Next, Charles Mann, no longer slipping and sliding around, sacked Elway for a nine-yard loss. On third down, running back Tony Boddie dropped a short pass; and on fourth down, the Broncos punted. Then the massacre began. On the Redskins' first possession, Williams connected with Sanders for an 80-yard touchdown pass. The PAT was good; the score was 10–7, in favour of Denver. On their second possession, the 'Skins ended a five-play, 64-yard drive with a 27-yard touchdown pass from Williams to wide receiver Gary Clark. The PAT was good; the score was now 14–10, in favour of Washington. Meanwhile, Elway had thrown five incomplete passes, and kicker Rich Karlis had missed a 43-yard field goal attempt.

On Washington's third possession, Williams completed a 16-yard pass to Clark just one play before Smith ran 58 yards for his team's third score in less than 10 minutes. The PAT was good again; the score was 21–10, Washington. The fourth possession began with Williams throwing an incomplete pass (and nearly an interception) up the right sideline, intended for Sanders. It ended with a 50-yard touchdown pass up the same sideline, to the same receiver (Sanders). The PAT was good; the score was 28–10, Washington.

Their fifth possession of the second quarter came as a result of an interception by defensive back Barry Wilburn. It was Wilburn who had been burned earlier by Broncos receiver Ricky Nattiel, for Denver's first (and only) touchdown. With equal footing however, it was no contest. The interception set up a 76-yard drive that ended with Williams tossing an eight-yard touchdown pass to tight end Clint Didier. With that pass, the FBQSSB tied the Super Bowl record for most touchdowns (four), held by Terry Bradshaw of the Pittsburgh Steelers since 1979. There were 58 seconds remaining in the first half when the Broncos got the ball back. They kept it for about 50 seconds before Elway threw his second interception of the half (both in the 'Incredible Quarter' – IQ for short). With 7 seconds remaining, the FBQSSB fell on the ball, mercifully ending the IQ. The score was 35–10 in favour of Washington, and there was still another 30 minutes of football to go. No team in Super Bowl history had ever scored more than 21 points in a championship quarter, or 28 points in a half. One had to wonder if the security guards posted outside of the Broncos' locker room door would be able to keep the team from submitting the remainder of their game plan in writing, and just getting back on the airplane for Denver, and calling it a day. I think I would have given such action serious consideration. But perhaps that's one reason that I'm not an NFL head coach. Still, what the *hell* kind of pep talk do you give a team that's down by 25 points at the half? Hmm?

The halftime show would have done Corinne Griffith proud. She was a well-known actress in the days of silent film. In 1936 she married George Preston Marshall, president of the Boston Redskins. Not only did she convince her new husband to move his football team from Boston to Washington, she also wrote the team song, 'Hail To The Redskins', and suggested the 'between-halves show' for which Redskins games became famous. Soon, all the other teams followed suit, and the halftime show became a pro football standard. At Super Bowl XXII, it featured 44 Rockettes (the famous dancers, from Radio City Music Hall in New York), 88 pianos, a 400-piece swing band, and Chubby Checker singing 'Let's Twist Again, Like We Did Last Summer' while dancing atop a giant, make-believe jukebox. 'The musicale represented the quiet, understated good taste that has become the hallmark of the Super Bowl,' said the *L.A. Times*. Ha!

By the time the second half was ready to begin, the television and radio announcers had described the game so far as 'startling' and 'bizzare'. One prognosticator (who, after Denver's sudden first quarter lead, pointed out that no team had ever won a Super Bowl after trailing by more than seven points at *any time* during the game) exclaimed, 'Who would have believed *this*!?!' The IQ had left several million mouths agape.

The third quarter was relatively uneventful. The Broncos had returned to the game hopeful, even optimistic (*how* did they do that?). But it didn't matter. Elway's incompletions continued to pile up. Ten of his 14 third-quarter pass attempts were incomplete, with one interception. 'There were tipped passes, hurried passes, frantic scrambles, dropped passes. Elway could do little right, and his team followed his lead.' There was, for all intents and purposes, no Denver running game. They gained a grand total of three yards in the third quarter. Meanwhile, the Redskins were cruising along, cushioned by a substantial lead that was about to increase. With 12 seconds remaining in the quarter, Gary Clark took a hand-off and ran 25 yards up the left side of the field. The fourth and final quarter opened with Timmy Smith (on his way to a record-breaking 200 yards-plus performance) running three consecutive times – 32 yards, seven yards and four yards – for his team's fifth touchdown. The score was now 42–10, Washington.

The Broncos' final possession reflected how their entire day had gone. Elway was sacked twice and threw one more incompletion. Then his team was called for two successive penalties, and finally had to punt. And that, my friends, was all-she-wrote for the Denver Broncos. All that was missing was Don ('Dandy Don') Meredith (a recently retired, long-time 'Monday Night Football' announcer) singing (?) 'Turn out the lights, the party's over, they say that all good things must end. . . .'

For their part, the Redskins evidently decided that a 32-point lead was comfortable enough for them to show a little mercy. So, after methodically driving the ball downfield from their own 25-yard line to Denver's 14, rather than run it in for yet another touchdown, or even kicking a 'chip-shot' field goal, the 'Skins let the clock run down on their record-shattering Super Bowl XXII victory. Washington had now won two Super Bowls in three appearances in the 1980s.

The Denver Broncos, on the other hand, had gained the dubious distinction of suffering back-to-back Super Bowl losses in the 80s, both by a blowout (19 points in '87; 32 points in '88). One more appearance this decade (and one more loss) would qualify them to be the 1980s edition of the 1970s Minnesota Vikings, who went to the Super Bowl four times – 1970, '74, '75 and '77 – and lost it four times. 'If I wanted to picture in my mind the worst thing that could happen to us,' said Broncos defensive end Andre Townsend, 'I would picture this.' Owner Pat Bowlen was quietly angry. 'When the other team scores 35 points in a quarter, you obviously have to look at your defensive scheme,' he said. 'And it isn't like just one guy got beat. Everybody got beat. Losing is one thing. Getting embarrassed is another.' Defensive co-ordinator Joe Collier avoided post-game interviews, hurrying away from the locker room. The 19-year veteran assistant coach had been under tremendous pressure all year; his defence was small, slow and inexperienced.

It was rumoured that Redskins head coach Joe Gibbs had been offered the vacant Green Bay Packers position, if he wanted it. He didn't. His team had just stormed its way into the history books. His players had just set or broken 14 Super Bowl records, including most net yards (602), most touchdowns (six), most points in a quarter (35), and most rushing yards (280). Doug Williams broke Joe Montana's 1985 record for passing yards (331) with his 340-yard air-show, and tied the record for touchdown passes (four), held by Terry Bradshaw of the 1979 Pittsburgh Steelers. Timmy Smith broke Marcus Allen's 1984 record for rushing yards (191 with the L.A. Raiders) with 204 yards, and Ricky Sanders broke Lynn Swann's 1976 record for receiving yards (161, with the Pittsburgh Steelers) with 193 yards, including the 80-yarder that tied the record for the longest Super Bowl reception, held by Kenny King of the 1981 Oakland Raiders.

Following such a magnanimous event as the Super Bowl, the President of the United States traditionally telephones the winner's locker room to offer his congratulations. Then, the citizenry of the winner's hometown – this time, it was our nation's capital – begins preparing for the return of their heroes. In Washington, which was already in the midst of a boisterous, exuberant celebration, there would be a victory parade on Tuesday. The team would meet with the President, bring him the obligatory Super Bowl souvenirs (usually a cap, a game ball, and a jersey with the number '1' on it), and then appear with him on the White House lawn. There was even a special, one-time shipment of Wheaties distributed only in Washington, with Doug Williams's picture on the box.

The Redskins' off-season would be filled with public appearances, product endorsements, and book deals. There would also be several renegotiated contracts – Doug Williams,

Ricky Sanders, Gary Clark, Timmy Smith, and Dexter Manley among them.

All of the fame and glory, the recognition and, of course, the money, made everyone forget for a moment about the battles that had been fought before and during the 1987 National Football League season; and about the war that was still to be decided in the courts. Players, owners and fans alike were all rejoicing together. All, that is, except for the people of Denver. What's worse – no football, strike football, or Broncos Super Bowl football? Hmm. Tough choice.

Chapter Twelve

'There is often pain in waiting and winning, as Doug Williams has learned over the years, and realised again in Super Bowl XXII,' wrote Mike Downey in the *L.A. Times*. His road to the winners' circle was a rocky one, strewn with seemingly insurmountable barriers and cruel twists of fate. But, through it all, Williams emerged standing straight and tall and said, 'I'm blessed.' He has endured all of the difficulties in his life with grace and dignity, and now enjoys a view from the NFL mountaintop. And the view is very, very good.

It began at Chaneyville High School in Doug's hometown of Zachary, Louisiana. He was called 'the Rifleman' because of his powerful throwing arm, and tossed 22 touchdown passes in his final season alone. He was offered a scholarship to Grambling State University by its legendary head coach, Eddie Robinson, which he accepted without hesitation. He was the third-string quarterback until the fifth game of his second year, when he seized the opportunity and led his team to a 21-0 victory over Tennessee State University. From then until the end of his college career, Doug Williams was Grambling's starting quarterback. During that time, he threw a touchdown pass in 39 of his 40 games; 93 touchdowns in all, and 8,411 yards, all school records that remain unbroken.

In college, Doug was the first quarterback from a predominantly black school to be named to the AP All-American team (outstanding college players chosen by Associated Press sportswriters around the country). A little over a decade later, in Super Bowl XXII, he made NFL history as the first black quarterback to start in a Super Bowl (FBQSSB). Said Doug, 'My whole life, whatever I was, I was "the first". It was destined.'

In Tampa, Doug was the toast of the town for most of his five years there. You see, before his arrival, the Buccaneers had managed only two victories (in 28 games) in the team's two-year history. In Doug's rookie year, they doubled that total, winning four games by mid-season. In all, they won five games (before injuries and inexperience overtook them) and lost 11. Still, it was their best season to date. The progress had begun, and the future looked bright. In 1979 Doug led his team into the playoffs, for the first time in their existence, with a record of ten wins and six losses. The Buccaneers had been the butt of tactless jokes not long before (it was said that Williams should be sent to Iran; he'd overthrow the Ayatollah), but this was their Cinderella year. In their first-ever playoff game, the Buccaneers beat the Philadelphia Eagles, 24–17, bringing themselves just one victory away from a trip to the Super Bowl. But then, the clock struck twelve, the horse-drawn carriage turned back into a pumpkin, and the Tampa Bay Buccaneers came crashing back down to earth, when they not only lost, but were shut out of, the NFC Championship game, 9–0, by the Los Angeles Rams. Doug injured his arm in the third quarter and had to leave the game. It was a bitter loss.

The Buccaneers returned to the playoffs two more times in the next three years, moved primarily by Doug Williams's arm. Yet, when his contract expired in 1983, and he asked for a raise, the club refused to pay him. He said it was one of the lowest points in his life: 'In '83, after five years, I started going through a lot of hardships in Tampa, and management decided not to pay me. They told me I wasn't worth what I was asking for. That showed me that they really didn't care what I had done in the last five years.' So he left. 'It took so much out of me. I gave them everything I had.' Was it racism? Many observers thought so. 'I never had to say that that was the reason, because I had so many other people who'd say it for me. And the funny thing is, it's not all blacks who have come to me and said this. I have a lot of white friends who say, "Hey, the only reason they don't want to pay you is because of your colour." A lot of people say that. But look at Tampa, and think about the people that they have had since Doug Williams left, and the amount of money that they have paid over the last five years. Compare what they have done in Tampa in the last five years to what Doug Williams did in the first five.' Hmm.

Another of the hardships that Doug struggled through while in Tampa – and by far the most devastating – was the loss of his wife, Janice. Just two and a half months after the birth of their only child, Ashley Monique, and ten days before their first wedding anniversary, Janice died after undergoing sudden emergency surgery for a brain tumour. She had been his college sweetheart, his best friend, his soulmate. 'I was in shock,' he says. 'I couldn't believe it was happening. . . . If I ever needed an excuse to be an alcoholic or a drug head, Janice's death was it. You never get used to death. But somehow I was strong enough to overcome it.'

When Doug left Tampa, no other NFL team wanted him. So he jumped leagues, and signed a five-year, $3 million contract with the Oklahoma Outlaws of the USFL. One year later, in December 1984, the Outlaws merged with the Arizona Wranglers franchise, and moved to Phoenix. One year and eight months after that, the whole league folded. Doug went home to Zachary.

Redskins' head coach Joe Gibbs had been the offensive coordinator at Tampa Bay when Doug first came into the NFL. He had been instrumental, in fact, in making the quarterback the Bucs' first choice. In August 1986 Gibbs again called on Doug, this time to ask him if his ego could handle being a backup quarterback with the Redskins. Said Doug, 'There were no starting jobs available in the NFL, and the Redskins were the only team that called me. What else was I going to do?'

He sat on the bench for the entire 1986 season, except for one play (an incomplete pass) in one game. But Doug was just happy to be in an NFL uniform again. He didn't mind backing up starter Jay Schroeder. Then, in 1987, Schroeder became consistently inconsistent. On 15 November, after repeatedly overthrowing open receivers, he was yanked from the game in favour of Williams. Doug came off the bench, threw two touchdown passes, and led his team to a 23–19 victory over the Detroit Lions. He had earned the starting job. Eleven days later, he sprained his lower back in practice, causing him to miss one game. Schroeder stepped back in, and gave one of the best performances of his career, winning back the starting job. Doug was so upset that it brought tears to his eyes. He said it wasn't because he wasn't starting, but 'because of a lifetime of frustrations'. He got another chance, however, when Schroeder proved ineffective against the Minnesota Vikings in the last game of the regular season. Once again, Doug came off the bench and rallied his team to an overtime victory. And once again, he earned the starting quarterback job. This time for good – or at least until the 1988 season begins.

If you believe, as I do, that life is full of God-ordained opportunities disguised as problems and challenges, then you will surely agree that Doug Williams has had more opportunities to grow than the average Joe. Even on the biggest day of his professional life, Super Bowl Sunday, the FBQSSB faced a couple of pretty tough challenges. First, there was the abscessed tooth that forced him into a dentist's chair for three hours of root canal surgery on Saturday – the day before the big game. 'There was some soreness,' he said on Sunday evening, 'but I didn't think about it today.' Right. Then there was that moment towards the end of the first quarter, just before the Redskins found their rhythm, when Doug slipped on the wet field, stumbled, fell, and twisted his left knee. He tried to walk back to the huddle, but collapsed in obvious pain. Joe Gibbs and everyone on the sidelines got a bit nervous. 'The guys knew I was hurting,' Doug said. 'But they also knew that I would hang in there.' After two plays, he was ready to get back into the game. 'I felt that if I could walk, I could set up. And as long as I could stand and set up, I wasn't going to let any pain keep me off the field.' Doug hadn't changed into longer cleats as most of his teammates had, and that may have saved him from a disaster. His knee was hyperflexed (stretched), but still stable. He returned to the game with a brace on, just in time for the IQ, and led his team to a decisive – a very, very decisive Super Bowl victory. Later he reflected: 'Through all the frustrations in my life, I've realised it could have been worse. I have a lot more than most people. I've been lucky and blessed.'

Chapter Thirteen

The 1987 NFL season left in its wake several genuine survivors, and a few notable casualties. In Green Bay, Packers head coach Forrest Gregg 'resigned' after four years at the helm. The Packers finished the season with a record of five wins, nine losses and one tie, bringing Gregg's four-year record to 25 wins, 37 losses and one tie. Two weeks later, on 14 January, he announced that he was accepting the head coaching job at his alma mater, Southern Methodist University. Now, you figure this: Forrest was trading the headaches, politics, and money of professional football for the headaches, politics, and lesser money of college football. SMU has not had a football programme since the 1986 season, when it got into deep trouble with the National Collegiate Athletic Association (NCAA) for recruiting violations. So here we have Coach Gregg, taking a $200,000 pay cut, and vowing to rebuild his alma mater's scandal-rocked football programme. Hmm.

In Los Angeles, Tom Flores bit the dust after nine years as the Raiders' head coach. Al Davis announced Flores's 'retirement' on 20 January at an elaborate press conference at the L.A. Airport Hilton Hotel. In attendance were several suit-and-tie clad current and former Raiders players. Flores had been with the club for 22 years as a player (quarterback), assistant coach, and finally head coach. His nine-year regular season record was 83 wins and 53 losses, plus two Super Bowl Championships (following the 1980 and 1983 seasons; records: 11–5 and 12–4 respectively).

There had been a 'general master-plan' when Flores took over in 1979, calling for him to coach the Raiders for ten years; and he had set a personal goal of winning 100 regular season games in that time. But, following an 8–8 showing in '86 (the club's worst record in 25 years), and an even worse 5–10 season in '87, he would have fallen short of his goal even if he'd decided to stay around for one more year. Rumour has

131

it that Tom was pressured into 'retiring'; that he was, in fact, fired as head coach. Not so, said 'Big Al' Davis: 'No one asked Tom Flores to retire. This is what he wanted to do. It was his decision.' Said Flores: 'I just feel it's time for me to step aside.' (Frankly, I think he got a little nudge.) Besides, as both Davis and Flores assured us, Tom would not be leaving the organisation altogether. Though we're not quite sure just *what* he'll be doing, we're told he'll serve as an advisor on 'special projects'. Asked what advice he would give his successor, Tom replied, 'Just win, baby.'

So, now, the question of the month was, 'Who will hire the NFL's first black head coach (FBHC)?' You could bet your life that the Packers organisation would not take such a precedent-setting step. Green Bay, Wisconsin is not one of our more progressive cities in terms of race relations. And since the team is run by a 'citizen-committee' of stockholders, there are two chances – slim and none – of them selecting the FBHC. Al Davis, on the other hand, has long been a trend-setter, has often bucked the system, and will usually do the unexpected. He was the odds-on favourite to hire the NFL's FBHC. Twenty years ago, Al's Raiders became the first team to select a black quarterback (Eldredge Dickey) in the first round of the draft. When he was commissioner of the American Football League, Al hired the first black official. There are two black assistants on the Raiders' current coaching staff, and the head coach for the last nine years (Flores) is a minority, a Mexican from a family of field workers. So, no one can criticise Davis on matters of equal opportunity (and the little plug by Commissioner Rozelle, about hoping Al Davis would consider hiring a black coach, could be construed to imply that, if he didn't, he's a bigot like the rest of them). Still, he will not be pressured into anything. Not race, colour, creed nor even sex has ever interfered with the idea of winning,' he said. 'I want the best people, and I'm going to choose the best person I feel can lead the Raiders organisation.' Al's choice turned out to be 35-year-old Mike Shanahan, the offensive co-ordinator for the Denver Broncos. Shanahan brought another Denver assistant coach with him – line coach Alex Gibbs – to be the Raiders' assistant head coach. That Al broke with his 22-year tradition of hiring from within the organisation was one thing.

That he went to the 'hated' Broncos was – well, un-expected.

Then there was Jimmy 'The Greek' Snyder. One Friday afternoon, while drinking his lunch at a well known Washington, D.C. restaurant, he was approached by a news team from the local affiliate of NBC-TV. During an impromptu interview, Snyder, a longtime sports commentator for CBS-TV, and a popular oddsmaker/football prognosticator, revealed to the interviewer (and shortly thereafter, to all of America) his confused theories of anthropology and history. Jimmy explained why blacks make better athletes than whites. Honest! He actually *said* this! 'The black is a better athlete to begin with, because he's been bred to be that way. Because of his high thighs, his big thighs that go up into his butt; and he can jump higher, and run faster. . . . It goes all the way back to the Civil War when, during the slave period, the slave owner would breed his big black with his big woman [notice the conspicuous absence of the word "man"?] so that he could have a big black kid, see? That's where it all started.' When asked about the lack of black managers and coaches in sports, Jimmy said, 'If they take over coaching, like everybody wants them to, there's not going to be anything left for the white people. I mean, all the players are black. The only thing that the whites control is the coaching jobs.' Well, officials at CBS moved quickly to distance themselves from Snyder's remarks, calling them 'reprehensible', and then from Snyder himself; he was fired immediately. Jimmy had also recently predicted that the Redskins would lose to the Minnesota Vikings in the NFC championship game because Washington's quarterback – Doug Williams, a black man – 'chokes' in the big games. After his Super Bowl victory, Williams, the game's MVP, replied, 'I've choked all the way to San Diego. That's fine with me.'

Remember the replacement players, the 'scabs'? Those 'talentless' shmucks who babysat the NFL while the 'real' players were away on business? Most of them were unceremoniously dismissed as soon as the strike ended. But some of those gems really got a chance to shine in '87, and when the final gun sounded on the strange season, they were still around. Take wide receiver Kelvin Edwards, for example. He was the fourth-round draft choice of the New Orleans Saints in 1986. He stayed there for one season, then was released after the 1987 training camp. When the strike came, he turned down strikebreaker contracts with the Saints, Chiefs, and Bears in favour of one with the Dallas Cowboys. There was an obvious need at the wide receiver position there, and he thought he'd have a better chance to shine in Texas. He was right. Edwards gave three sterling performances during Strikeball '87, catching two touchdown passes in his first game; grabbing a 62-yarder, and 100-plus receiving yards in his second game (which led to NFC offensive player-of-the-week honours); followed by another 100-plus-yard day in his third game. The result: an invitation to continue starting when the strike was over. Kelvin accepted, of course. When his new teammates returned from the picket lines (those that were left that is; the Cowboys 'boasted' the largest number of starters to cross the picket line), they treated him fine, he said. 'There wasn't any animosity when they came back. If there was, individuals kept to themselves about it. I don't feel like a "Carbon Cowboy" now. Then again, I never did. I just wanted to go out and play some ball.'

There were more survivors like Kelvin. Several replacement players around the league made the most of this 'last chance' opportunity to catch on (and stay on) in the NFL. They had survived previous rejections from other clubs; they endured harsh feelings and, in some cases, harsh treatment from striking players; and they overcame the odds. Nine of them ended up in the Super Bowl, three Redskins and six Broncos.

Anthony Allen, a wide receiver for the Redskins, played in the United States Football League until it folded in 1986. Then he joined the Atlanta Falcons, but tore up his knee, and was waived. Washington signed him for strikeball, and in three games he caught 13 passes for 337 yards, including 255 in one game. But he was waived again when the strike was over, only to be re-signed when starting receiver Art Monk got hurt. Like Kelvin Edwards, Anthony said the hard feelings from the striking veterans didn't last very long. 'You earn their respect on the practice field, not in replacement games.' With a little luck, the 'replacement' tag will soon disappear. 'I think it will probably go into next year,' said Anthony. 'Maybe after we go through training camp and make the team again, it might die out then.'

Bibliography

The following sources were used as reference for material in this book:

The League: The Rise and Decline of the NFL, David Harris
The Sports Encyclopedia: Pro Football, David S. Neft and Richard M. Cohen
Government and the Sports Business, Roger G. Noll
Private Antitrust Litigation, Barry Kellman
History of the Sherman Law, Albert H. Walker
Law and Economic Policy in America, William Letwin
The Official National Football League 1987 Record and Fact Book
Sunday Mayhem, Richard Whittingham
About Three Bricks Shy of a Load, Roy Blount, Jr
Sport Magazine
Sports Illustrated
Inside Sports
Sporting News
New York Magazine
Los Angeles Times
New York Times
Washington Post
USA Today
New Orleans Times Picayune